NEW MOON ASTROLOGY

*Lunar Cycle Mastery, How to Say "I Told You So", &
Spiritual Energy Meditations*

ANGELA GRACE

Ascending Vibrations

CONTENTS

CLAIM YOUR *BONUS* MANIFESTING TOOLKIT

Are you done with settling for a mediocre life, wasting precious time, & ready to live your wildest fantasies?

• Hack your brain, boost performance, & release blocks holding you back from greatness

• Awaken this amazing energy to supercharge your manifestations

• Stop wasting what little precious time you have on ineffective methods

Manifesting Toolkit Includes:

1. **Supercharged Manifestation EFT Tapping Video** Download To Banish Limiting Beliefs & Propel You Toward Your Dream Life (Infused with 432 Hz Frequency)

2. **Secret Formula Journal** Daily manifestation Ritual Done For You. Simply Rinse & Repeat At Home. (You Can Print This Out, Stick On Your Wall, & Cross Off The Days You Complete The Ritual)

3. **Powerful 10 Minute 'Shifting Your reality' Guided Meditation** MP3 Download (Infused with 528 Hz Frequency)

4. ***BONUS*** LOA boosting 10 Minute 'Feminine Energy Awakening' Guided Meditation MP3 Download

Go Here to Get Your *BONUS* Manifesting Toolkit: **bit.ly/manifestingforwomen**

INTRODUCTION

What do you feel when you look at the Moon? Do you just admire its beauty and mystical presence in the sky or do you feel a deeper connection? I am guessing that it is the latter which has brought you here. You are right, as the Moon does hold special powers and comes with a great energetic field that affects all creatures on Earth. It moves eternally in orbit around the Earth and influences the water, nature, animals, and human beings on so many different levels. The whole presence of the Moon is magical, transcendental, and filled with amazing secrets waiting to be unveiled.

Have you been feeling super excited under the full moon? Do you often find yourself drained of all energy when the Moon is not there for you to see? Although you might find it hard to believe, the Moon and other celestial objects can have a dramatic impact on your life. They can affect you emotionally, physically, and mentally. So you can feel depressed without any solid reason or your mood can be lifted in an instant instead. Sometimes you get an energy boost, while at other times within a lunar cycle you feel down and need to rest. So many people miss out on their full potential because they cannot understand what is going on in their life. They feel estranged by nature, out of tune and completely alone.

However, you can totally harness the energy of the Moon and use it to your advantage! You don't need to remain idle and suffer through these energy fluctuations every month, and you should not go through these changes without trying to interpret them. Instead, you can take matters into your own hands and benefit from the mystical power of the Moon. On top of that, you can master the art of astrology and find out how the planets, the houses, and the zodiac signs can work in your favor. You can do so much, just by learning how to work around the lunar cycle and adjusting your actions accordingly.

Rather than fighting with the different moon phases, flow with them and understand what they mean. Comprehend how you must change your behavior and set your intentions exactly when the Moon is just beginning a new journey around the Earth. See why you should rest after completing each cycle and why it is of such great importance to recover, regain your strength, and start fresh. See how you can release anger and fear, letting go of any blockages that hinder your spiritual path. The universe is wise and perfectly balanced; you just need to find a way to align with the cosmos to supercharge your life!

Bathe under the moonlight and feel its energy surrounding you. Why would you settle for a life that is dependent on external factors, when you can take control of those factors and use them to find harmony in your life? Focus on your personal growth and walk steadily towards self-awareness. The Moon is your ally, as long as you let it work its magic. In this book you are going to find everything you need, so that you better understand the secrets of the Moon. There are abundant benefits in going with the flow of the cosmos, allowing the Moon to shine brightly into your existence, and changing your entire standpoint. Have faith in these glorious powers and trust in the universe, for it has been there forever.

Whether you have always dreamed of becoming a contemporary witch eager to cast your spells to promote your happiness, or you are just curious about your cosmic powers, this book will definitely enlighten you and fill you with gratitude about the world. I am sure you can't wait to start mastering the lunar secrets, so let's get started... I am wishing you the best of luck on this wondrous adventure that you are about to begin. Join me and let's shoot for the Moon!

MOON PHASE MASTERY: YOU ARE HOLDING THE KEY TO UNLIMITED POWER

The Moon is the absolute epitome of mysticism and romance, inspiring us ever since the dawn of ancient civilizations, and filling us with a transcendental sensation to cherish. As the Sun sets and darkness spreads across the world, it is the Moon that guides us along with thousands of stars scattered in the sky. People in love always turn to the Moon for help, for courage, and inspiration. They even resort to the Moon for guidance when all hope is gone, such as unrequited love or a condemned romance that cannot have a happy ending. But when the happy ending comes, it is the Moon that illuminates the most spectacular moments spent by those hopelessly romantic souls.

Every writer has found endless inspiration by gazing at the Moon and its different phases, while poets have created their best forms of literature motivated by its enchantment. Painters have dedicated their finest masterpieces to the Moon and the eerie atmosphere it so beautifully complements. Unlike the Sun, there is something unworldly about the Moon that makes it even more thrilling to look at.

Although we gaze at the sky every night, what we see changes in a pattern that allows us to dream away and imagine the secrets of our origins. It is a mystery we are all drawn to, in pursuit of conquering the truth and learning more about this astonishing element of the solar system.

Without a doubt, the Moon has played a great role in our culture and nature itself. The Earth would not be the same without its largest natural satellite orbiting around it, never stopping for a moment. What would happen if it did stop? The entire universe would be thrown out of balance, causing world-shaking events. Luckily, we can all rely on the Moon to maintain that precious balance and continue worshiping its mystical nature. We will continue celebrating its milestones, anticipating the glorious full moon, and observing the subtle silvery slivers as they form in the sky with each new moon.

Although the Moon is such a fundamental part of our very existence, the truth is that there are things about it we simply don't understand. In fact, many may think that the Moon stands still or that it is bright on its own. There are those who believe that some days the Moon simply doesn't appear in the sky, and others who do not realize that there is much more than what meets the eye in the various shapes of the Moon. In this chapter, I am going to show you what those moon phases really mean and how to interpret them. As soon as you unveil the mysteries of the Moon, you will gain knowledge that will enable you to fully comprehend the special power it holds. It is an exciting adventure, I promise!

UNDERSTANDING MOON PHASES

Why is the Moon visible on several days of the month in its full glory, whereas others you can barely see it? Well, unlike what many people might think, the Moon does not change shapes. It is always there, orbiting around the Earth and leaving its everlasting mark on us. So what happens? First of all, take a moment and think about the distance separating us from the blazing Moon: It is 35,000 kilometers away, floating in space, and offering mystical features and tantalizing beauty. What might come as a surprise is that the Moon itself is pretty dark! In fact, it resembles asphalt and it is equally reflective, too.

The Sun is responsible for illuminating the Moon, which in turn shines bright down on Earth. It is the Moon's strategic position exactly between the Earth and the Sun that allows it to glow like that! It is also spherical in shape and orbits around the Earth. So, the way we see it up in the sky every single day depends on where it stands at that time. On the bright side, literally speaking, the Moon is always half-illuminated by the Sun. It depends on the direction from which the Sun is shining over the Moon and the angle from which we get to observe from afar. The only thing that changes is the way we look at it from the Earth, causing those moon phases we all know and love.

Now, a full orbit of the Moon around the Earth takes about a month (29.5 days to be exact). As you can see, there is a striking resemblance between the words 'moon' and 'month', revealing that mystifying connection. So the beginning of the orbit represents the new moon. This is when the Earth, the Moon, and the Sun are all in alignment, and the Moon is as close as it can be to the Sun. As a result, the Moon is up during the day, although we cannot see it. At that point, we face the unlit half of the Moon and therefore we do not quite understand its presence in the sky. Sometimes, there might be a small silvery slice, but it is very subtle.

After a few days, we see that the Moon has traveled eastward, and it now allows us to see a crescent Moon. As the days go by, the crescent becomes bigger and bigger. This is what leads us to a "waxing crescent" Moon. After having covered one quarter of its orbit, the Moon is now about 90° away from the Sun. The 'terminator', meaning the line that divides the Moon in its illuminated and dark side, is now right in the middle. This might confuse you a little, as we have only covered the first quarter of moon phases. But as the Moon continues on swinging around, we move forward to the "waxing gibbous" moon phase. This is when the Moon appears swollen, hence the name.

Perhaps the most mind-blowing time of the Moon's orbit comes 15 days after the new moon. The Moon has now traveled half the distance of its orbit and now sits right opposite the Sun and the Earth. At that point, the Sun fully illuminates the side of the Moon and offers us one of the most amazing phenomena in the world. This is the "full moon" phase. Due to its position, the Moon now rises at sunset and sets at sunrise. The result is the astonishingly bright Moon we enjoy throughout the night. The full moon has inspired people for ages, and now you know how it is formed!

But then once again, the Moon continues on its course around the Earth and starts getting closer to the Sun. The same phases will take place, but in reverse. As the illuminated side becomes smaller, we enter the "waning gibbous" phase. The Moon is still shining brightly, but it slowly begins shrinking and its dark side gets bigger. A week after the full moon, the terminator is again slicing the Moon in two equal parts. We have entered the third quarter of the orbit, and in a few days we will observe the "waning crescent." Finally, after having traveled 360° around the Earth, the new moon is here, in anticipation of another thrilling lunar journey.

In Alignment With the Moon's Energy

As the Moon orbits around the Earth, it controls its rhythms to a great extent. It is no secret that the Moon influences the water reserves on the planet, while the Moon's gravity causes the tides at sea (Choi, 2017). Take a moment and think of the analogy that we are made of water as well. So it makes perfect sense that the Moon influences humans on a deep, cellular level! This is a connection nobody can question; why you feel differently during the full moon, or any other phase of the Moon that has a direct impact on the universe.

The new moon offers an opportunity to set new intentions and start over again. It represents new beginnings, and there is so much potential that you can gain out of each new moon cycle. Recharge your body, mind, and soul under the omnipresent lunar power and get ready for what lies ahead! Even if you feel introverted, you should not worry! When the new moon comes, it is only natural that you seek some time alone to regain your strength, think about what has happened, and envision the future. Along with the waning crescent, setting new intentions becomes even more necessary. Plant the seeds of your dreams and wishes, so that you watch them grow. What would you like the universe to bring? What do you want to manifest in life? After having regained your strength, now you are ready to conquer what is yours by right!

In the first quarter, you may see some sort of resistance when it comes to the realization of your dreams and wishes. This should not let you down, as you now have the necessary power to overcome the obstacles and continue on your course toward accomplishing your intentions. Although there might be a few bumps along the road, this does not mean that you should give up or settle for less. The Moon is on your side, as long as you let it. Work hard and prepare to reap the benefits of your determination.

If need be, the waxing gibbous allows you the time to reassess and refine your actions accordingly. There might be times when the best thing for you is to modify your goals and set different intentions. Of course, no one is invincible and you should keep that in mind. Dreaming big is always a great thing, but at some point you must adapt to reality and make the most out of any situation. As the full moon approaches, you should be strategic and make sure that you harvest the fruit of what you have planted at the beginning.

During the full moon, things get tense and you may experience emotions that you cannot fully grasp or justify. Try not to get overwhelmed, because it is the lunar energy that drives them. Be open to receiving everything you have worked so hard to achieve during these past two weeks. This is the best time to watch those intentions come to life! At the same time, you will get new opportunities and you will realize that there are so many wonderful things for you to achieve. The world is filled with such potential and you need to be open to receive.

As the waning gibbous is formed, this is the time to feel the most grateful. You have already acquired what you wanted and you should be feeling extremely happy! Therefore, you should practice gratitude and express your positive emotions toward everything that has happened in your life. It has been an extraordinary journey and you have received abundance in all its forms, so now you must give thanks and share your enthusiasm with the world.

Any negative thoughts or bad events that have been dragging you down should be released. Let go and forgive others.

Do not hold on to any grudges, as something like that will poison you and eat you up from within. Instead, feel free to let go of your anger and do not consume your mind with such petty emotions. You should be looking upward, not downward! Finally, with the waning crescent you are free to surrender and take rest. This has been an intense lunar cycle, and you have benefited from its unique opportunities. You have received everything and now it is time to enjoy what you have acquired. Rest for a while, as a new cycle is about to begin with the new moon.

ACTIVATING YOUR POWER INFUSED ONENESS WITH THE MOON

Mankind has always been drawn to the Moon. Early humans observed this breathtaking celestial object in the sky and wondered what it represented. Philosophers looked at the Moon as the natural boundary between the Earth and heaven above. Our ancestors managed to determine the differences in nature according to the moon phases. This was monumental, as it enabled them to adjust to the distinct behavioral patterns of their prey, for instance. Consequently, humans were capable of surviving through the important findings that the Moon provided for them.

If you go back to Egyptian mythology, you will see that the Egyptians worshiped Khonsu. He was the God of the Moon, and his name literally translates to "the traveler" (World History Edu, 2020). This is a direct reference to the travels of the Moon, orbiting around the Earth. So, our ancestors had realized long ago that the Moon is not static, but instead moves in a continuous path that affects everything in the universe. Respectively, in Greek mythology, you will find Artemis, who is not only the Goddess of the Moon, but also the Goddess of wild animals and the wilderness as a whole. This reflects how ancient Greeks had also fully comprehended the immense impact of the Moon on all living things and nature itself.

Along with the Egyptians and the Greeks, ancient Babylonians managed to calculate the exact time it takes for the Moon to complete a full orbit around the Earth. More than that, they also took into account the slight orbit of the Earth around the Sun, and this is why their solar lunar calendars are so accurate! Incredibly, thousands of years ago, people were successful in determining what modern scientists would only calculate through the help of cutting-edge equipment and a wealth of knowledge stemming from observation. The Roman Goddess of the Moon is called Luna, revealing again how strongly the ancient civilizations believed in the power of the Moon.

When it comes to the weather forecast, the Moon can be of great help. When the Moon is high up in the sky, it affects the overall amount of rainfall. It does so by creating bulges in the atmosphere, which in turn interfere with the rain forecast (Hickey, 2019). Ever since antiquity, people have looked up in the sky and interpreted the Moon in order to identify several weather patterns. Since they used the Moon as a calendar, they marked its changes, and predicted how animals and nature as a whole would react. For instance, they saw the full moon as the time when animals would become more aggressive. This was a clear sign that they had to adapt, rather than miss out on the opportunity to outsmart their enemy.

It was a matter of self-perseverance for people back in the day to observe even the slightest changes in the lunar cycle, as well as any other changes in nature. This way, they managed to create a collective memory of the overall power of the Moon that was passed on to the newer generations. Although some of it might seem superficial or even superstitious, in reality it is the outcome of years and years of distilled observations. The Moon is much more than a centerpiece in the celestial decor and this is depicted in many cultural records that have survived throughout the centuries.

So we have already established that the Moon holds a special power over nature, and that this power has been made aware to humans even from the early days of civilization. However, what about humans themselves? What special power does the Moon hold over you and me? It makes total sense that we are also affected by the lunar cycle, but in what ways?

IMPACT OF THE MOON ON HUMAN BEHAVIOR

The Moon exerts gravitational force on everything in the universe. This includes the oceans, which explains why the Moon has an impact on the tides. Keeping that in mind, it makes absolute sense that the Moon holds a special power over humans. As well, we are mostly composed of water (up to eighty percent). What you should know is that the Moon's orbit around the Earth is completed in an elliptical pattern. This means that the two celestial objects do not have the same distance between them at all times. When they are closest together, this is called 'perigee.' On the other hand, when the Moon and the Earth are farthest apart, then this is called 'apogee.' The impact of the Moon on human behavior is directly associated with this very distance.

One more way in which the Moon affects human behavior is sleep. Maybe it is because on some days of the month, the Moon shines brighter and therefore alters our circadian rhythms. Be it as it may, no one can argue with the fact that some people are gravely affected by the Moon and get deprived of a restful sleep, especially right before or during the full moon. This of course is in perfect alignment with the moon phases, and particularly with the new moon offering an opportunity to rest and recover from the intensity of the entire lunar cycle (Grover, 2021).

The glow of the Moon is crucial, though, for the survival of several species. From sea creatures to deer and other animals, the lunar cycle offers a great way of knowing when to look for a mate, as well as when to go hunting. The tides of the sea can help move the eggs of some species to a safer environment. But how can the animal kingdom know? How do eels and corals, fish and turtles, reindeer and other mammals understand when is the right time? Do they have a built-in clock synchronized with the Moon and its phases? It seems that the Moon acts exactly like a signal, supercharging them and stimulating them to act as they do.

One of the main reasons why some ecosystems have been out of balance might be attributed to artificial light. Unlike the past, or any natural landscape away from the hustle and bustle of modern civilization, we have nowadays become accustomed to non-stop illuminated environments. However, there are many species out there that have absolutely no idea how to deal with these changes! They are thrown off guard and nature's balance is threatened. You might see it yourself, if you take a moment and really look at the world. In fact, you may even experience it in your own everyday life. Why do you find it hard to relax, sleep, let go? Why is stress so overwhelming?

Another connection that has remained controversial over the years is the menstrual cycle. Menstruation typically comes every 28 to 30 days, while the lunar cycle is completed every 29.5 days. As such, there is a time overlap between the two. If you take a moment and think about what menstruation represents, you will recognize that there is a new cycle of life celebrated every month. Those who menstruate can become fertile and bear the fruit of this fertility boost, before finally taking a rest and starting all over again. If you recall the lunar cycle, this is exactly what happens to the Moon. So there is definitely a bond between the two, at least conceptually.

If we get to think about it, there is a specific time in the lunar cycle when everything seems to blow out of proportion. Emotions can be magnified and people feel affected by something out of their control. This, of course, is the full moon, and a specific phenomenon that has inspired mankind, bringing a lot of conflict between those who believe in a deeper connection and those who remain skeptical. Which side are you on? Let's have a closer look at the impact of the full moon on us humans, putting emotions aside and focusing on what actually happens.

How About the Full Moon?

How often do you look up and marvel at the bright, full Moon? Are you convinced that it holds a special power over you, or do you believe that you are simply romanticizing this celestial phenomenon? You are not alone in this question! But over time, people have used this correlation to interpret signs and justify specific behavioral patterns. Have you ever watched wolves howling at the full moon? This is classically misinterpreted, since in reality wolves tend to howl even during the day, and follow a specific pattern. They look up in order for their howling sounds to spread further away, and in order to communicate with their pack more efficiently.

The full moon enhances everything that you already are, feel, and want. It heightens your senses and allows you to conceive things that would otherwise be too subtle to even realize. During the full moon, every trait of yours becomes magnified! Be it a positive or a negative attribute, it does not matter. What matters is that the full moon expands it and makes it more prevalent than it would otherwise be. At the same time, you may be feeling things too much. Yes, that's right; the full moon intensifies each and every single feeling! This is the reason you may feel saddened and filled with despair, without even knowing why. Anxiety, depression, as well as several mental illnesses spike during the full moon.

Since the Moon ultimately drives your emotions, it makes perfect sense why these emotions would be at their peak when the full moon approaches. We are biologically programmed to be affected by natural phenomena and this is one of the greatest in the world! As such, this is reflected in the way we feel and experience things. When you are in love, the full moon makes your heart beat faster and you long for moments of intimacy with your partner. When you are sad, you get even gloomier as the Moon gets brighter.

Maybe it has to do with our perception of the world. Since our senses are heightened and we are on alert, we turn to introspection. We take a look at our life and become more critical of it—disappointed even—when there is really no ground for such negativity. Perhaps it is the fact that we have been led astray from our true path that we get reminded of it at the full moon, which is extremely discomforting and fills us with self-doubt. In a time when nature gets in perfect alignment, we feel out of place. We feel like we do not belong and this is a rather disheartening feeling.

The full moon has been associated with lunacy ever since ancient times. In fact, this is why there is such a deep connection between the Moon (hence 'Luna' in Latin) and the disturbing mental state of being insane. Such people have been called lunatics, closely related to the Moon and its immense impact on human feelings and, ultimately, their actions. In the past, people believed that somehow the full moon made the world more aggressive and violent. They were convinced that crime rates increased dramatically at that time of every moment.

Even if such theories have been proven wrong over the

years, they still influence people. There is a strong cultural belief that the full moon wreaks havoc upon the world, leading to irrational behavior and promoting aggression, violence, and similar negative emotions. The full moon seems to have an impact on how we feel and this is not always a good thing! In the past, a lack of knowledge resulted in superstitions about the Moon, especially when it was the brightest in the sky. People watched animals more clearly during the night and therefore they thought that the full moon drove their behavior, enabling them to threaten humans. But it was most likely the other way around.

When a blanket of thick darkness covers everything around you, there is a lot that remains unseen. This does not mean that it is not there, it merely means that you cannot fully comprehend its presence. When the full moon comes, it unveils those mysteries of darkness and brings clarity.

WHAT ARE YOU WAITING FOR?
HOW TO EASILY TRANSFORM
YOUR LIFE WITH MOON PHASES

The Moon is the mother of the universe, representing the feminine power of the cosmos, whereas the Sun represents the masculine forces that infuse the world. These two are completely balanced, existing in perfect harmony with each other. The Moon enhances our bodily rhythms. During the dark or new moon, you can cast spells and set your intentions for a new beginning. If you wish to take a new path, this is the best time to schedule it! This is a productive time in the lunar cycle to sow the seeds of your ambitions, successes, and dreams, projecting them to the universe and allowing them to shape into reality.

Every lunar month depicts the time duration between two consecutive new moons. It is otherwise known as a "synodic month" and covers 29.5 days. There are people who mistake the synodic month for the "sidereal month." A sidereal month is a month that covers the time it takes for the Moon to circle the Earth, or 27.3 days. This is understandable because they both measure the same thing, practically. However, the sidereal month does not take into account the subtle orbit of the Earth around the Sun. This means that every time the Moon orbits around the Earth, it does so in an elliptical shape and that messes with the calculations a little. Consequently, the Moon has to move a little more each month to catch up with the Earth, leading to the synodic or lunar months.

With the new moon, this celestial object appears dark and empty. Gradually it gets filled up with light and brightness. Until you are completely illuminated by the abundant shining of the Sun, the Moon asks you to make the necessary changes to welcome this glorifying phenomenon up in the sky. You must generate light by yourself, so as to get perfectly aligned with the Moon and communicate with each other on a deeper level. This all happens in the period of the waxing moon, which is when the Moon increases its brightness and the surface that is covered with light. Put action into everything you wish to fulfill, and behold as you watch it unfold before your eyes. It takes some effort, but this effort is definitely worth it.

In the waxing moon, you should accumulate strength and make sure that you are on the right track. Extend yourself and prepare yourself for the most promising time of the entire cycle, which is three days prior to the full moon. You have already planted the seeds and now is the time to nourish them! Water them, so that they can grow and offer you their precious fruit during the full moon. It requires some time, so you should not get discouraged if a lunar cycle passes and you still have not reaped any fruit.

There will come a time when you benefit from your efforts! What you should focus on is the proper balancing aspect, though. Even if you put your whole heart toward achieving your goals, you must remember to rest and recover at the same time. It is not a sprint race you are training yourself for, rather than a continuous journey resembling a marathon. You risk feeling depleted and completely out of balance, drained of energy and determination. You do not want that, because you need your strength to claim what is rightfully yours!

During that time, there is an excellent 'pranayama' (practice of breath control) that you can follow! In this pranayama, you focus on sharp breaths through your nose. What you're aiming for is to get full contractions and releases in the abdominal area. When you inhale through the nose, the abdomen releases the air; when you exhale, the abdomen pulls in the air. The entire scheme should feel like a pump. You need discipline, in order to complete this, feeling the air in your lungs clearing your body and your mind. The more you do this pranayama, the more energized you will instantly feel.

Along with this pranayama, you can also do an energy 'mudra' (gesture) to succeed in your goals during the waxing moon. Touch the two middle fingers of each palm to your thumb, keeping the other three fingers stretched apart. Let those palms face upwards toward the sky and the Moon, while you close your eyes. In this way, you prepare yourself for new beginnings. You reset and get filled with energy, while also focusing on your intentions, and even getting clarity on what those intentions should be! It does not matter if you keep your hands at the level of your heart, or if you rest them on your thighs. This mudra works either way.

Visualize what you wish to accomplish in order to be able to project it to the world. Through this mudra, you concentrate on your goals and you clear the path for them to become reality. They will be fulfilled, as long as you remain on alert and pay attention to your needs, your desires, your dreams. You must have faith and nurture yourself, so as to embrace these new goals. Relax while you are keeping your eyes closed, picturing where you are after during this lunar cycle. You will feel heat generated, along with energy from within.

This is perfect, as it means that you're motivating yourself toward promoting these goals of yours! When you feel complete, bring your hands in front of your chest at heart level, palms pressed together. This is a gesture of gratitude, giving thanks to yourself. Just remember to do your pranayama and mudra daily during the waxing moon period, up to 100 exhalations at a time to achieve the optimal results. Calm down and visualize what it is you want, making space to put action into it, acknowledging that there will be challenges along the way.

There are moon cards available for you to buy and make use of, in order to maximize the effect of the Moon on your life. Once you purchase a moon deck, typically consisting of 44 cards, you can use them to set your intentions and remain focused on them. In fact, you have the option of using such cards to interact with your intuition, and developing a deeper connection to the universe surrounding you. Each card comes with its own mantras, as well as insights, and useful information that facilitates the whole understanding of the Moon and the universe.

FLOWING WITH THE DYNAMICS OF THE MOON

Women tend to be more in-tune with their emotions than men. Without a doubt, this is a stereotype that does not cover every single individual on Earth. However, it does hold some ground. Women and men, due to differing expectations, have learned to deal with feelings differently. Women are generally in deeper alignment with their feelings, and it may come easier to express themselves as individuals. It is worth noting that feelings stem from one's soul and they are genuine representations of your very existence. They offer a glimpse into the person's heart and mind, a glimpse of truth in an ocean of lies.

Emotions can be traced in the transits of the Moon on a person's chart. According to the specific place of the Moon every single day, or more accurately every single night, the person may experience turbulence in the way they feel. Since the Moon agitates the water element, it is responsible to a significant extent for the way we express our emotions. If you want to control your emotions, you need to learn how to grow a healthy relationship with the Moon and adhere to its powers. Mondays are supposed to be ruled by the Moon, as this is the day that highlights its energy! Therefore, this is the perfect time to fast, if this is something you're interested in. As a result, you will be in an elevated state of awareness. The same goes with the full moon.

One of the best mantras for the Moon is "Om Chandraya Namaha", which you can repeat 108 times or more to conquer its unique energy. In this way, you will be able to find a gateway to your very existence. As you will realize, the Moon represents so much in the world. First of all, it represents your mindset. This means that it reflects your thoughts and your own perception of your life. What do you believe about specific things? What is your opinion about several aspects of the world? Next, the Moon represents your mother and the relationship you have with her. Lastly, the Moon represents your home. The place where you feel secure and safe, your personal sanctuary of calmness.

So, the Moon is ultimately the Goddess of Light, Luna,

who drives you toward living a sustainable, fulfilling life. The Moon shines brightly upon you and offers you its mystical powers to expand your existence, and create the life you have always wanted. In order to achieve that, you must connect with Luna truthfully, without any obstacles getting in the way which prevent you from experiencing this special bond. You must do that consciously, with your whole heart and soul. Find a quiet place and create the perfect environment to promote the connection.

It is imperative that you create a sacred space where you can invite Luna to connect with you on that deep level. Unlike what you may think, there is an option for you to have such a place always available to you. No matter where you are, you can establish an etheric structure of light as a mobile sanctuary of light, connecting to the Moon regardless of any physical barriers present. If you want to activate this etheric structure of light, you must remain calm and be open in a receiving mode. Close your eyes and breathe deeply a few times, so that you can relax and let go of all tension.

Once you have come to such a state, you are ready to state what you want to create! More specifically, you can say something like this: *Temple of Moonlight, activate all around me. Below, above, up and down, create a safe sanctuary of light.* While you are saying this, visualize this sanctuary gradually forming around you. Allow enough space inside the structure in order to feel comfortable. It is archaic in shape, with tall pillars and radiating a purple color, emitting high frequencies. Imagine yourself surrounded by this magnificent sanctuary, and you will instantly feel like a huge burden has been lifted off your shoulders.

You can activate that temple on a daily basis, bringing it with you every single moment of the day and always keeping it available. Upon having established such a safe place, this is where you wish to invite Luna to connect with you. Do that and allow her to come in her human form: A woman, a radiant woman, that comes into your personal shelter and connects with you, shining her beautiful essence down on you and allowing you to become a part of her. As you continue on invoking her and getting to feel her close, you become more empowered and you feel that strong bond that has been created between the two of you. Indeed, this is a timeless bond beyond dimensions and it only grows stronger!

Interpreting the Past With the Power of the Moon

There are many people who feel haunted by their past lives. They sense that there is a deeper connection between what they are experiencing right now and what they have already experienced in their past lives. There seems to be a behavioral pattern, which is often attributed to karma. It is true that there are past experiences that form your behavior and channel you to make choices in life. No one can deny that humans are a species of habit. We are drawn by familiar things and this is why we seek uniformity, in order to feel safe. Intimacy is a wonderful aspect for us and therefore we tend to choose what we know over the unknown.

Take a moment and think for a while about yourself and the choices you have made so far in your life. Have they been based on a pattern? I presume you have understood by now that most of your decisions fall under the same principles, and you can somewhat predict what is going to happen in the future based on your past. Although this is not concrete and there is always the possibility of breaking the cycle, chances are that your actions are more or less aligned over time. You might feel threatened by that lack of originality, even though you may also feel relieved.

Karma is basically the notion of unresolved issues from past lives. So, based on what you have experienced before, you choose a life form and a path that is aligned with the past that allows you to maintain a specific course. According to evolutionary astrology, there are behavioral patterns that we seem to repeat no matter what in our lives. Even if these patterns are not beneficial to us, even if they hinder our progress and prevent us from experiencing life to its fullest potential, we still go ahead and make the same mistakes over and over again. Why would something like that happen? Why do we sabotage our lives?

The basic evidence of the existence of past lives lies within a simple yet indisputable observation: Imagine a girl who has grown up in a family where she suffered abuse. Her parents were alcoholics and had outbursts of anger. She grew up in a hostile environment, unable to establish safety and love. It is likely that she always felt out of balance, out of place, and she wanted a way out of this greatly discomforting reality. Although she grew up and became independent, she continued being drawn to those who resembled her parents in more ways than she could even admit to herself.

This feels like a pattern, like a self-fulfilling prophecy in the field of psychology. It is like you can almost foresee what bad thing is about to happen in your life, before even going down that road (Ackerman, 2018). The truth is that you feel comfortable in that pattern, because you have been used to it all this time. I am not referring only to your childhood and the early traumas you might have experienced at that sensitive period of your life. On the contrary, I am talking about all these past lives you have completed so far. Now you are conversing with the universe, asking for another try. This time you will do better, you will be better, you will tackle the challenges much more efficiently than before. Could there be more eloquent proof of past lives?

Now, let's try something cool that will tip you off as to how old you really are! Are you wise after having lived on Earth for countless years, or are you just setting out on your cosmic adventure? Do you want to find out how many lives you have had so far? Let's invoke the power of numbers, or 'numerology', in order to find out! First, get the number of the month when you were born. If it is a single digit, such as April, the 4th month of the year, simply keep this in mind. If it is December, the 12th month of the year, then add 1 and 2 together to get the number 3. Do the same with the day on which you were born. If you were born on the 2nd, you would get number 2. If you were born on the 14th, though, you would add the digits 1 and 4 to get number 5.

Finally, add the digits of your birth year and hold on to the number. For instance, those who were born in 1982 would get 1 plus 9 plus 8 plus 2. In other words, they would get number 20. Then, you are ready to find out the exact number of your past lives. Take the number of your birthday, your birth month, and your birth year together and add them. If you get 11, 22, or any digit from 1 to 9, then this is the total of past lives you have had so far. Otherwise, if you get any other double digit, add the numbers until you get a single digit. For example, if you come up with 42, then you should add 4 and 2 to reach 6, meaning you have had 6 lives so far.

4

THE LAW OF ATTRACTION ON
STEROIDS: MANIFESTING
MASTERY WITH THE MOON
PHASES

I am sure you are all familiar with the Law of Attraction: If you manifest positive thoughts and emotions, then the universe will return them to you. The same goes for negative emotions, however, so you should be extra careful as to what you project to the world (Lopez Simpson, 2017). The Law of Attraction is a magnificent concept, allowing you to receive all the blessings you want to see in your life, as long as you remain focused and have patience. Of course, the elements of nature play an important role in this process. The Moon is a celestial object holding extreme power, which makes it a great asset in your hands to manifest what you want to attract in your life.

Are you under the impression that you can only manifest during the full moon? Untrue! You are luckily able to do this throughout the lunar month, making use of the different phases to attract literally anything your heart desires! Luna, the Goddess of the Moon, is right by your side at all times. Even when you cannot see her, she is there guiding you to reach your highest self and live your life exactly the way you have always dreamed of. First of all, what makes it so special to manifest with the Moon? By now, you should know just how powerful the Moon is. Its energy is so unique, and therefore having the opportunity to use this magnificent power to supercharge your manifestations seems purely awesome!

Your spiritual self in collaboration with the eternal power of the Moon will definitely accelerate your manifestations, as long as you work around the moon phases and adjust your spells accordingly. In order to manifest with the Moon, all you need is proper time to dedicate to yourself. There is no need to rush into things, so you should find some time to concentrate solely on your manifestations. In addition, you should have a piece of paper or your journal throughout the entire process. Of course, you will need a pen or pencil to write with. If you wish to immerse in the calming experience of Moon manifestation, then some calming music in the background will work wonders along with some scented candles or incense.

It is great if you can combine the powers of the four elements into your manifestation. Obviously, by following my previous advice for burning candles or incense, you have the element of fire. Then, you can place windchimes to gather the element of the air into the room where you are about to manifest. For the element of water, a wonderful piece of advice would be to get a small water fountain, or make use of an essential oil diffuser. You can always add some ocean water to a cup or a bottle, or manifest while in the bathtub. Finally, you can capture the element of earth by bringing a plant or a rock in the room. Of course, you can always enhance your experience with the help of crystals and precious stones.

There are many other wonderful details that can make a difference in your manifestations. For instance, everybody holds some possessions that mean something special to them! A ring that has been passed on to you by your grandmother, a scarf that your best friend brought back from a cherished vacation, a picture of a loved one, or even the nostalgic aroma of your favorite cologne! All these elements can play an important role in your manifestation and can increase its power. Apart from that, you might feel creative and engage in putting together a vision board. There is nothing more stimulating than keeping everything neatly organized on a board, serving as constant reminders of what you wish to accomplish in life. Just let your imagination run wild! Use colorful markers, scraps from old magazines, post-it notes, paintings, and anything that makes sense to you! Turn to the vision board for inspiration and you will enjoy the energy boost every single time.

In my book, *Manifesting for Women*, I have delved into the mysteries of manifestations and I have included valuable information about how to meditate, journal, and practice gratitude and visualization in the most efficient manner possible. It would make me happy to see that you followed these guidelines towards reaching the highest levels of manifestation, and have received everything you have desired in life. I promise, there is so much more to this than a couple of affirmations and a journal! Once you play your cards right, you see how it all comes together and the results are purely mesmerizing. Your life has so much potential and it is a shame not to claim what you are entitled to experience. Just reach out, be open, and welcome this magnificent journey that has just begun for you.

WISHING ON THE MOON

Each phase of the Moon holds a very special power, and you should take advantage of these phases in order to make the most out of your manifestations. With the new moon, you know that you plant the seeds and you set the intentions for the entire lunar cycle. This is when you should write down what you want to happen in the next month, so that you project it to the world and the world responds back to you! It is important to remain calm and safe in your personal sanctuary. As the new moon starts its journey towards reaching fulfillment, you must focus on your wishes and manifestations. Be detailed and consistent, subtle yet conscious of your choices and be determined to make them real.

With the waxing crescent, just dig deeper and put some effort into those intentions. Work towards making them happen! This is not just wishful thinking and staying idle. On the contrary, you should put some pressure behind your entire endeavor and watch the magic unfold. Stick to your journal and make a list of those intentions, as detailed as they can be. This brings us to the third part of the lunar cycle, which is the first quarter of the Moon. At this point, you need to turn this list into an actionable plan. What can you do to forward your plan? Be strategic and think outside the box! Keep your mind on the end goal and make sure that you do everything within your power to accomplish that.

After doing all that hard work, we now shift over to the waxing gibbous phase of the Moon. Three days before the full moon arrives, you must get into a receiving mode. This is when you can use visualizations, so that you actually see how these intentions are going to look as they enter your life. If you are determined to rest more, then you can start visualizing the impact this rest is going to have on your body and mind. *See* your face radiating with glow, as you have just enjoyed a great night's sleep and you are filled with energy. *Feel* that rest taking over you and hold on to that feeling.

At last, it is the full moon and you have received what you have been waiting for throughout the lunar cycle. During the full moon, the energy is at its highest level and you want to take advantage of that any way you can! Upon receiving all those lovely intentions you have set at the beginning of this lunar cycle, you should now express your gratitude. You are thankful to the universe for what you have received, and you are especially thankful to the Moon for helping you achieve your success. It is now the time to sit down and write a gratitude list. Let go of any doubt that you may have been holding on to all this time, and as you let go, simply enjoy the abundance that has been brought into your life.

Now the Moon is beginning to go into the waning gibbous phase. This is the time to become conscious of what you have. Reflect on what you have accomplished so far. The waning gibbous phase is very important, as it allows you to see what you have been lacking. Assuming that you have not received what you wanted, there are certain limiting beliefs to blame. Now is the time to reveal these beliefs, so as to overcome them and pave the way for our next intentions. I know that you may be tense when you explore the fear and doubt that has been keeping you from accomplishing your goals. However, no matter how hard it might be for you, it is necessary that you look deeply into your most intimate places and find these limiting beliefs of yours. After all, they are undesirable and you do not deserve them.

During the next phase of the Moon, the third quarter, you can transform those limiting beliefs into your most valuable assets. This is a great feature, turning something negative into positive. "What doesn't kill you makes you stronger", to quote Friedrich Nietzsche (Wohns, 2020). Use the lessons that you have learned up until this moment and see the silver lining. Push forward, unleash your power, and watch yourself grow even further through these obstacles that you have been forced to overcome! Shift your focus and modify your behavior, so that the specific limiting belief you used to have does not touch you any more. Be careful, though, because you do not want to simply ignore the limiting belief. Hiding it under the rug just won't do you any good.

A mere 72 hours prior to the new moon, we have entered the waning crescent phase of the moon. You must have accumulated a lot of energy throughout this great adventure! In fact, it is highly likely that you are feeling a little overwhelmed by this process. So now is the time to empty all this energy and prepare yourself for the dark beginning of the new moon. Release the tension, let go of the manifestation you've created, and make room for the new intentions that you are going to sow in a few days. You may hold on to the precious experiences, but you must release all the energy that you have put into it. Otherwise, you would feel exhausted and you would have no will to start over.

The new moon represents rebirth. In absolute harmony with one's menstrual cycle, this is the exact time when you will begin a new journey towards creating a new life. Even though the new moon is dark, there is an illuminated side of the Moon always shining bright in the universe! It is up to you to wait until it is revealed to you once more. Remember that your intentions should be clear and honest, coming from the depths of your soul, reflecting who you want to be and what you want to do at any given time. You should only focus on what actually matters to you and no one else. This is your life, so you must paint it in your own true colors.

Whatever you do, it is important that you practice gratitude and thank the universe for your blessings. In today's world, many people forget to do that, and they believe they are entitled to everything without giving anything back. Nothing could be further from the truth, however. The laws of the universe are everlasting and omnipresent, governing the planets and celestial objects, humans and all living creatures. We are only a tiny fragment of this universe and we are expected to cohabitate in harmony with the rest of the world.

It is a matter of understanding who you really are and what you are meant to do in the world. The universe will listen to your calling, but will only respond to those who appreciate what they receive. If you wish to be abundant in life, you need to give thanks for all the prosperity that comes your way, while appreciating the fact that you have been blessed with so many things. Do not forget or underestimate the importance of gratitude. By doing so, you comprehend the very essence of the world and deeply realize the core of existence. You are meant to be happy, but you ought to understand how fortunate you are, and show your respect, your gratitude, your thanks towards the eternal powers of the universe.

Sometimes we get discouraged by the fact that our intentions are not successful during the lunar cycle. I have heard over and over again from people that the Moon might not be as powerful as they had initially anticipated. They do not understand that the universe truly sees inside you, and does not grant your wishes unless they come straight from the heart. Moreover, there are intentions that are far more complicated than others. As such, it will require more time for these intentions to be turned into reality. In this case, what you need to do is be patient and welcome change as it is formed.

Following the moon phases, before the lunar cycle ends, you must show the Moon how appreciative you are of what you have received throughout the month. It doesn't matter if you have successfully achieved your goals or not. Each cycle offers unique lessons, and you need to keep your eyes open in order to acquire that precious knowledge that will serve as future wisdom. For instance, you may have discovered what has been holding you down in the form of limiting beliefs. What has prevented you from pursuing your career ambitions so far? Who has been pulling you down, discouraging you from actually realizing your dreams and desires?

Be truly passionate about manifesting! Believe it in your

core that you are destined to succeed, and this is exactly what you are going to do. Unless you set your intentions with that in mind, you cannot expect them to be brought to life. The universe needs to know that you are strongly energized about these intentions in order to program their realization. Through passion and commitment, you build your armor and you show the world how much you want to attract all these marvelous things into your reality. After all, when you believe that you already have that abundance in your life, your frequencies become elevated and this is projected to the universe around you.

Let's Talk About Love

Love makes the world go round, right? Who could ever imagine a world without love, without affection, without that unique bond between two people that defies dimensions, expectations, and limitations? That uplifts your spirit and creates a bond that cannot be broken? One who has not yet been loved has not yet realized the beauty of being alive. I know that romance has been praised throughout the years, and we have all grown up waiting for the moment when we would meet that unique person who would connect all the missing pieces. For when we meet that person, our life would then make sense, and we would have the perfect reason to enjoy every single moment together.

For some, this all sounds idyllic, and sometimes people stop believing in love. They are either too afraid to let go and trust others, or they feel that they do not deserve to spark such intense emotions. Of course, everyone deserves to love and be loved. When you meet that person who you have been waiting for all this time, you cannot stop giggling and you feel butterflies in your stomach! The world is finally smiling back at you and you can look forward to even more wonderful moments ahead. Who wouldn't want to welcome pure bliss into their soul?

Yet, along with love comes heartbreak, jealousy, unrequited love, and pain, like you have never experienced before. The intensity of emotions is earth-shattering and makes many people swear that they will never love again. They feel an emptiness that resembles no other, and grief after the loss of someone dear. How can they cope after such an immense change? Many choose to remain numb, shying away from even the slightest form of love that might make them feel something again. Of course, others may choose to stay in the game and continue on their journey towards finding true love.

Whether you have already found your significant other or you are still looking, it goes without even saying that love is always in the air. It doesn't matter if you choose to ignore it, love's dynamics are simply too intense. Obviously, you can manifest love into your life or you can improve your current relationship through moon rituals. Nature is by your side; all you need to do is ask. But before moving forward with the specific moon rituals that can bring you closer to your love interest, you must realize that it all boils down to your relationship with yourself.

No matter how frequently you do those rituals, unless you fully comprehend that a loving relationship starts from within you, chances are that you will never experience it. If I were to ask you right now what love means for you and what the first thing that comes to mind about love is, what would you answer? If the answer is a specific person, then you may need to make a shift in your mindset. You should focus on yourself, because otherwise you may be sabotaging yourself, and you would be hindering your progress towards finding that true love.

In a way, your romantic partner is the mirror of your deepest self. Even though it is easier to believe that you are not getting the love you need because another person is not giving that to you, the real culprit is yourself. Once you dig a little deeper, you will see that your relationship (or the lack thereof) is a reflection of the way you hold the love energy from within you. In fact, your entire existence is the reflection of your inner energy pattern. If you believe deep inside that you are not worthy of being loved, then what you get in real life is a manifestation of this belief. It is awful, but it is the truth. Of course, this does not affect your possibility to create superficial relationships. As soon as the relationship tends to get more serious, your insecurities and feelings of worthlessness emerge.

I hope you are determined to reverse that situation and allow yourself to be loved. In order to do that, I want you to take a piece of paper or write down in your journal all these things that you would expect your significant other to offer in your relationship. For instance, you can write: *I want my partner to bring me flowers*, *I want my partner to talk sweetly to me*, *I want my partner to express how proud they are of me*, or even, *I want my partner to love me unconditionally, without judgment*. All these things reflect how you want others to treat you and especially the person you love the most.

Well, having completed the list, it would be good to go over it and read each and every single thing that you have written. Once you do, start treating yourself like the partner you desire. Show yourself the love that you deserve, the love that you are entitled to in life. Start buying flowers, take the day off, go out for a spa treatment, stroll leisurely down the park, and watch your favorite movie. Do whatever makes you happy, so that you feel loved—by you! This is the secret to unlock unconditional love by others.

One more thing that you need to remember is that there is a cosmic timing for everything to happen... and the universe knows it! Even if you are in a hurry and want to meet the love of your life right away, this might not be the right, divine timing for you. As an entity, you are much bigger than what your mind is able to understand. You are part of the universe and therefore you should adhere to its rules, waiting for the perfect timing to come. I can sympathize with the concept of wanting something to happen right now. However, you should control your urges and resist that feeling of despair. This is now who you are deep inside.

What you want to manifest should come to you effortlessly, as part of the natural flow. Take a moment and think of all the times you got what you really wanted. If you look carefully, you will see that more often than not, you were not even paying attention! You did not pursue what came your way, but you welcomed it as an unexpected gift. It took you by surprise and this made you feel even more wonderful. How many times was this a manifestation of your urges? How many times did you think: *Oh I must have that NOW!* and the universe responded immediately by giving it to you? I am guessing that this has never happened in your life, as it has not happened in mine either.

When it comes to moon love rituals, you should work around the lunar cycle and take advantage of the different phases. The new moon of every month is the time when the Sun and the Moon are in conjunction. They are together, creating a divine portal that enhances the actual power of your manifestations. So during the new moon, you should clear your mind, rest, and meditate. Focus on the present moment, appreciate it, and then write down a list of your desires. Remember that you need to project these desires in a positive manner. Rather than saying, *I want this person to love me*, you should say, *I am an expression of divine love and I am worthy of being loved*.

As soon as you have this list complete, you should keep it somewhere safe and protected. You can choose to put it in an altar, on your bedside table, or even within your daily journal. After a fortnight, there will be a full moon. This is the time when the Sun and the Moon are actually opposite to each other. Similarly to the new moon, this is also a very powerful time during the month. Whatever seed you have planted now is going to flourish. So, you need to be careful and look out for those manifestations of your set intentions. If you don't see anything, then you must search for blocks that hinder your progress.

A full moon ritual also involves meditation. You should pick a nice and quiet place, bathed by the light of the full moon. Sit comfortably with your palms on your knees facing upwards. Start breathing deeply, inhaling the divine love and exhaling those blocks that stand in the way. After completing this full moon ritual, you can write a list of everything that you would like to acquire during the full moon. Have another look at your new moon desires and see what has manifested into your life. Be very open and flexible, as this is a never-ending process. Sometimes it takes a lot more lunar cycles for an intention to become reality. This is the beauty of life, so embrace it and cherish every moment!

5

HOW TO DROP JAWS AND SAY "I TOLD YOU SO" WITH LUNAR FUELED SUPER-ABILITIES

Are you interested in skyrocketing your intuition, predictions, and psychic abilities with the help of the different moon phases? I am sure you are! It is a fascinating journey around the cosmos that can boost your manifestations and welcome those gorgeous intentions into your life. You simply need to know where to look. The Moon is a powerful celestial object, influencing the Earth on so many levels. It governs the unconscious realm and intuition is part of that. Your intuitive mind is a sacred gift and the Moon allows you to connect with it deeply and strongly.

We are parts of nature, so it is only fair to assume that we are also affected by its magnificent power. However, how can you supercharge your abilities and increase the odds of inviting absolute bliss into your life? As the Moon orbits around the Earth and reflects the spectacularly abundant light of the Sun, it becomes a portal channeling vast energy. As soon as you understand how this energy is distributed throughout the lunar cycle, you will be able to maximize its effectiveness on both yourself and those around you. You will be capable of controlling your emotions and allowing them to flow naturally, as your intuition is speaking to you through them. If you are determined to delve into the mysteries of the cosmos and change your life based on the power of the Moon, then you need to interpret those signs, see when to act, and when to stay still.

First of all, let's focus on an essential part of everyday life. Intuition is directly linked to your personal happiness and self-actualization. It is an important aspect of your personality, driving you to act the way you do. This is what drives you to live life to its fullest potential, taking advantage of the opportunities that it has to offer. How can you trust your intuition, though? How can you be certain that it is not just your impatience trying to take over, leading you to catastrophic events of great proportions? With the guidance of the Moon, trusting your intuition will be exactly like returning home.

Intuition can be described as your inner voice, your gut, or that feeling of knowing something beyond a shadow of a doubt. This voice from deep inside you is attempting to speak to you, advising you as to what you should do. It is worth mentioning that intuition barely adheres to social norms or other rules that have been dictated by the world. It is that higher self of yours who is trying to communicate with you! Even if you are afraid to let go, it is in your best interest to reconnect with that part of yourself that has remained dormant all this time, due to those norms and other rules applied to you by society.

So as you can see, most people have neglected nurturing their intuition and truly realizing that it is there to guide them. Your goal should be to learn how to distinguish your inner voice—your intuition—and listen to what it has to say. Another interesting point of view is that this voice also repre-sents your ancestors guiding you, motivating you to push forward and become the best version of yourself! This is a wonderful notion, and is based on the eternal wisdom of the collective that is translated into your intuition. Through this voice, you are expected to break free from a vicious cycle that keeps you restrained and limits your potential.

I completely understand why there is so much doubt associated with listening to one's intuition. Since misinterpreting that voice happens more frequently than what I would like to admit, people get skeptical. They are critical of intuition, and some might even question its overall value in a person's life. Nevertheless, intuition is your constant motivator to progress and become the best version of who you really are. You should not underestimate its importance, as it is the fuel that sparks your existence and allows you to achieve greatness!

If you are concerned about whether or not to listen to your intuition, there are several things that you can do. Trust the power of the Moon and adjust your rituals according to the specific moon phases. This way, you will get optimal results. First and foremost, you can communicate with your deeper self through meditation, especially during the full moon. Meditate with the intention of giving space to your inner voice and discovering that intuition deep inside you. Whether you are at home in your personal sanctuary or outdoors, you can meditate after creating the perfect atmosphere. As we've discussed, you are more than welcome to burn some sage or light a scented candle, use wind chimes or listen to the therapeutic sounds of the waves, the wind, or water flowing.

After having created such a marvelous, welcoming atmosphere that promotes relaxation and enables you to feel comfortable, you can start asking yourself questions about yourself. For example, you can ask, *Who am I? How am I feeling now? Why am I unhappy today?* and similar questions that pop to your mind. Now, before any social monitoring takes place, your intuition is going to step up and answer. So once you hear your deeper self answering those questions, you know that you are communicating with your intuition. This is best performed in the new moon, when you set your intentions for the lunar cycle that has just begun.

You can do the same with any issue that has been troubling you for ages, such as, *Should I quit my job? What career path should I follow? Is my relationship healthy?* and so on. These are just a few of the questions that you can ask yourself to establish your connection with your inner voice. I am sure that you may feel a bit awkward at first. This is perfectly understandable, because you have never been encouraged to rely on that voice in your life! But if you ease yourself into the process and take some time, this will all flow naturally.

Besides meditation, you can also try getting out of your comfort zone! Set out on an adventure on your own and listen to what that inner voice has to say. Listen to that voice and do what it tells you to do, in order to evaluate the results at the end of the day. Chances are that you will have achieved something out of the ordinary, something that has made you feel great about yourself. Last but not least, indulge in art, but remember to avoid any agenda. For instance, take a piece of paper and a pen (or a pencil) and start free writing. Do not think about it; just let those words flow naturally. Try abstract painting, freestyle dancing, or whatever works for you.

Through these amazing activities, you can get in touch with your intuition! Explore the powerful effects the Moon has on your own existence and delve into its presence deep inside you! Be gentle and do not beat yourself up if you do not succeed in listening to your gut right away. It may take a few lunar cycles to open up and prepare yourself to accept this mental shift, to embrace your most creative, intuitive, and emotional self. All those years you have suppressed its intensity and this is why it has remained hidden in the darkness, shying away from communication. Remember to avoid all judgment, and do your best to feel like a child again. Perhaps this was the only time when you were in absolute alignment with your intuition, as no social norms got in the way and prevented you from listening. Don't worry, you will get there!

PREDICTING THE DIFFERENT MOON PHASES

How can you be certain when it comes to the specifics of a lunar cycle? How can you tell, beyond any doubt, that tonight it is the waxing crescent phase, or that three days from now there will be a waning gibbous phase? Well, there is always the internet and no one can argue that *Google is your best friend*. Going online, you can easily use any interactive tool that allows you to identify the exact phase of the Moon on that particular day! For instance, you can see that the Moon is at four percent of a waning crescent upon looking it up (Sinnott, 2017). These tools are highly accurate, and they can even help you go as far back in the past as you wish for a deeper understanding of lunar cycles.

Even though technology has come a long way and you can get that type of information effortlessly, it is much better if you figure out yourself how to calculate the phases of the Moon. You already know that the Moon orbits around the Earth on a monthly basis, and this is the reason why there are such differences in the way we look at it from afar. This is an elliptical orbit, meaning that it is not one hundred percent circular. On the contrary, we also learned that there is a mild imbalance in the circle, and this leads to 29.5 days instead of the actual 27.3 days that it would take the Moon to orbit around the Earth in full cycle.

However, when you want to calculate the moon phases in the sky, you take into consideration that a full lunar cycle lasts 28 days. As we have seen, the actual cycle does not last 28 days, so take this with a grain of salt. Now, what you want to do is depict this cycle on a piece of paper. So, draw a circle and cut it into four equal slices, just like you would do with a pizza cutter. Then divide those pieces in two. In this way, you will get a full circle with eight equal pieces that you can number. Guess what? These are the lunar phases for you to remember.

If you want to have a clear perspective of this lunar cycle, then imagine cutting the circle into two with a horizontal line. Since the entire cycle lasts 28 days, it is only logical that half of it will be 14 days. So a full moon, which is number 5 in the numbered cycle on your paper, will take place exactly 14 days after the new moon. Respectively, if you are at number 2 (the waxing crescent phase) and you want to calculate where you are going to be in 14 days, then the answer is 6, or else the waning gibbous phase.

You may want to calculate where you are going to be in seven days' time. This is of course easy to predict as well, since what happens is that a lunar cycle will have moved a quarter of its course within seven days. Unlike what you might think, not all phases have the same duration! In this case, number 1 is the new moon and lasts for a single day. After that, there is the waxing crescent that lasts for six days. So upon reaching the eighth day of the lunar cycle, you will have reached the first quarter, or number 3. In a similar pattern, you can also calculate where you are going to be after 21 full days in the cycle.

Obviously, over time this gets easier to understand, and you become much better at predicting the various moon phases. Typically, with the help of this visualization of a cycle divided into eight equal slices, you will always be able to identify which phase you are on, and which phase you will be on in a time period of 7, 14, 21 or 28 days. Nevertheless, there are several other cool techniques that can aid you in your attempt to interpret nature and its marvels. Whether you are experienced in this, or you are a complete novice, you can work wonders with the right tools.

If you do not want to get into all that fuss, and assuming that you just do not care for visualizing the cycle in your mind, you can refer to a ping pong ball. To be honest, any white object in a spherical shape will do, as long as you can hold it in your palm. So go outside and look up in the sky on a clear day, approximately an hour before sunset. You will have the opportunity to spot the Moon then. What you need to do is hold the ping pong ball up to the sky, right next to the Moon. Since the Sun illuminates the ball from the same angle as it does the Moon, you will instantly see the specific moon phase depicted on the ball.

Are you more of a visual person? If so, then you can use your creativity and whip up something truly amazing! At the same time, your craft may help you get a better glimpse at the moon phases. You are going to need a white styrofoam ball and some black paint. Your next step is to paint half of the styrofoam ball black. While that dries, write down the different moon phases on a piece of cardboard or construction paper as they occur in a monthly cycle. Then, glue the styrofoam ball onto the center. When you glue the styrofoam, just make sure that the black side faces the new moon phase.

According to each phase, you can see the illuminated parts of the Moon appear in perfect harmony.

Slightly less complex than that, but equally inspiring, is the following method to predict the moon phases with great accuracy: You will need a white styrofoam ball again in order to complete your experiment. This time, the ball needs to be placed on top of a pencil or a straw. Use a lamp with a bright light to represent the Sun. The styrofoam ball will once again be the Moon. Once you stand facing towards the lamp, the illuminated part of the styrofoam ball that you are holding in your hands that represents the Moon is behind you. Therefore you cannot see it. Instead, you see the dark part of the Moon. Having that as a starting point, move in a circular manner and watch the different moon phases as they unfold on the ball.

Finally, you can create a moon slider to identify the exact moon phase you are on every single day. Use thin cardboard or construction paper and cut a large square, which you then fold in half When you unfold this, you will have a right and a left side. Make sure your cardboard or paper is relatively big,, because your next step is to draw the eight different moon phases. These drawings will be your point of reference. Identify the moon phases as you complete the drawings. Then, cut out a small circle in the middle of your circle. This is going to be your Moon! It is best if you use white or light-colored paper to construct the whole craft.

After doing this, you will need to get a black piece of paper. On one half, cut out the shape of a large circle, and on the other side, cut out a crescent. As the lunar cycle begins, place the black paper over your white paper, so that it covers the entire circle. While the Moon orbits around the Earth, watch its reflection in the sky and move the black paper to match that picture. The only limitation with this method is that you cannot depict the first and last quarter. Fortunately, they are quite easy to remember even without this special craft. So this is another technique on how you can tell which moon phase you are on without fail!

What Are Your Psychic Gifts Defined by the Stars?

Do you want to know what your psychic abilities actually are, based on your Moon astrology birth chart? There are many more than just a few, well-known traits attributed to you by your sign. In fact, there are amazing psychic gifts that the stars and the Moon shower down to you according to your exact birthday! Below, I am going to analyze those psychic abilities that you have been blessed with at the time you were born. Read along and see if these characteristics connect with you!

First of all, Aries comes with a fiery intuition. It is, after all, a zodiac sign representing the element of fire! You have been given the power to sense the perfect timing to start something fresh, and take chances and risks. Your intuition is definitely spot-on and allows you to modify your actions towards achieving your goals in the best manner possible. However, at some point, this intuition of yours might be mistaken with lack of patience. If you feel that you just cannot wait any longer, which makes you rush into a specific action, then this is probably a trait you must tame and try to control.

Representing the earth element, Taurus is able to rationalize things and remain stable. Being grounded gives you the best perception about everything that happens in your life, enabling you to avoid negative consequences that often stem from impatience and acting on the spur of the moment. Your psychic power has to do with a deep connectivity between yourself and your surroundings. You listen to the environment, and you get to decide how to act based on what you make of the situation at hand. Take a moment and think about the energy you get upon entering a specific room. This is your psychic gift projected to you, so do not ignore it.

Moving on to Gemini, here the element of air is omnipresent. Geminis are often clairvoyant, as they are gifted listeners and communicate with the universe on a deep, genuine level. You feel like your mind never ceases to function, which is absolutely right! Thousands of images literally pop into your mind non-stop, while your eagerness to learn and process every single detail enables you to channel spiritual messages. You are great at communicating with others, which offers you the opportunity to be creative and indulge in writing, speaking, and consulting.

Cancer reflects the element of water. It is a highly sensitive zodiac sign, meaning that you probably feel that you are overwhelmed by emotions at specific times within the lunar cycle. For instance, during the new moon, Cancers will feel the collective emotions flowing through them and charging them greatly. You have a special ability to connect to others' feelings and this makes you a great listener, as well as a unique person to empathize with. However, there are times when this gift seems to be overpowering you. This is when you need to remember that it is actually a gift and it is meant to heal others in moderation.

Returning to the fire element, now is the time for Leo to shine! What is so intriguing about this sign is the fact that it holds a deep connection not only with the Sun, but also with the Moon. It is the perfect combination of a dynamic personality, with great courage and determination, which at the same time attracts people with the magnetism of the Moon. So your psychic gift is none other than your charisma, your unique blend of attributes that makes you irresistible! You channel positive energy and people get inspired through your presence. Spread that energy into the world, because this is your calling.

Virgo is the second zodiac sign representing the earth element. You have the psychic power to be present in the moment and pay attention to the slightest of details. Even though some might claim that you always opt for perfection, you also remain grounded and communicate with the world in its very core. A great thing about Virgo is that they can tap into the divine knowledge and integrate it into the world. As a result, you can manifest ideally and you can use this psychic gift to naturally heal others. It is an amazing opportunity to bring the vastness of the universe into the three-dimensional world we live in.

Next, Libra is another sign ruled by the element of air. Libras are people who crave balance and do everything within their powers to smoothen any differences. They are able to see past the polarity that oftens leads to conflicts, since they realize the value of balance and harmony. Your psychic gift is to integrate dualities and bring balance to the world, appreciating the unique aspect of every single view. Upon recognizing a conflict, your natural instinct dictates that you resolve it without delay. You value the opposites and do not try to change anything, rather than only seeing the good and focusing only on that.

Scorpio is another water-ruled sign. In this case, you can see right through people and understand what they are actually made of. You cannot be fooled, since you are greatly intuitive and you read the energies quite naturally. To that extent, more often than not, a Scorpio will go away and try to hide from the rest of the world. They do not wish to reveal what has been revealed to them by others, as this might feel too intense. Furthermore, Scorpios are extremely sensitive and deep as a sign. This is why many become mediums, communicating with other dimensions. Besides looking out for yourself, since you are very vulnerable, you also need to realize your boundaries regarding spiritual trespassing.

Another fire sign of the zodiac is Sagittarius. If you have a Sagittarius Moon, then you most likely never lie about anything in your life. It is true that Sagittarians do not feel the need to hide things or mislead others. On the contrary, they are ruled by an immense feeling of optimism and they tend to light up the room as soon as they enter. You will find it extremely easy to manifest great things into your life, as your high vibrational frequencies allow you to do that easily. Your imagination runs wild and you are capable of vibrant visualizing. In addition, you motivate others and bring out the best in them.

Capricorn is another earth sign. Your psychic gift is that you are able to remain focused and determined in a single thing, away from any distractions. You are extraordinarily passionate about what you want to do and do not rest until you have succeeded. As a consequence, you are the best manifester in the entire zodiac! You have been blessed with a sense of deep, absolute knowledge as to what you must do in order to bring those manifestations into your life. By exuding such wisdom and maturity, you often become a role model or a mentor to others.

Moving on to Aquarius, there is a contradiction here. Although this is an air sign, it is represented by the water bearer. How cool is that? By fusing those elements together, you create an electric atmosphere. You are naturally connected to the universe, to what lies beyond. Your psychic power enables you to understand what happens in the world on a deeper level and comprehend the truth behind the lies. Because of your connection to the eternal power of the universe, you often astral travel or daydream. Finally, you have the ability to foresee the future and read through other peoples' intentions.

Wrapping up the zodiac sign, Pisces is indeed the last water sign, and comes with great mysteries waiting to unfold.

You are also greatly intuitive and you are in tune with the beyond. Your psychic gifts are relevant to your sensitivity. Because of your extreme receptiveness, you often get overwhelmed by the intensity of the emotions and you tend to try and escape. You feel what others feel and you experience clairvoyance. Moreover, you have deep compassion for others. If you have a Pisces Moon, you are introverted and shy.

☙ 6 ❧

WHAT THEY DON'T TELL YOU
ABOUT ZODIAC SIGNS

hat sign are you? is much more than a convenient line to start a conversation! Obviously, your zodiac sign has a great effect on your life. Whether you care to admit it or not, the planets have aligned in a unique pattern on your birthday and they have shined down on you their special powers! Floating in the sky in a perpetual dance with the stars and the other magnificent celestial objects, the planets have created a wonderful flow of energy and they have been imprinted on your existence forever.

Due to the complexity of the solar system, you cannot expect that a single planet or star affects you all on its own. On the contrary, there is an entire system that forms this sophisticated structure that allows you to grow and expand. As soon as you become aware of its power, you will be able to interpret your birth chart and understand how astrology defines who you really are. It is astonishing to see just how much you have been influenced by the stars, the planets, the houses, and the specific positions of each and every single celestial element!

Below, you will have the opportunity to analyze your natal chart and learn more about the details that you should pay attention to. Get a journal and start creating the foundations on which you are going to unveil all those mysteries of the universe... they all start with your zodiac sign!

HOW TO READ YOUR ASTROLOGICAL CHART

Unless you become familiar with the various celestial elements, you will never be able to fully grasp the magnitude of astrology. As a result, you will be constantly missing out on the marvels of the universe! If you are determined to understand how the Moon works and what effect it has on you throughout the lunar cycle, you must also pay attention to the planets and other celestial objects that surround the Moon and interact with it on various levels.

You do not have to be a professional astrologer, in order to comprehend astrology and its basic concepts. To help you, I have gathered here everything you may need to read and interpret your astrological chart. Below is all the information that allows you to delve into the mysteries of your birth chart, and understand how the planets, the signs, and the houses interact with each other. This is a wonderful collaboration—a planetary symbiosis if you will!

Before moving on, I highly recommend that you get a piece of paper or your journal, and a pen or marker to keep notes. First, divide your paper into three tables. You will have a column dedicated to the planets, another one to the signs, and a third one devoted to the houses. Now, you must be careful when you complete this chart. It is imperative that you write down everything in order, so that each planet is aligned with a sign and a house. Begin by writing down the Sun. This is an all-mighty planet that governs the sign of Leo and the fifth house. Of course, feel free to draw the Sun next to the word or scribble the zodiac sign next to its name!

Below the Sun, you get the Moon. The Moon governs the sign of Cancer and the fourth house. Continue writing down the planets on your table, keeping in mind that the following planets rule more than one sign: Mercury rules both Gemini in the third house and Virgo in the sixth house. In a similar pattern, Venus rules both Taurus in the second house and Libra in the seventh house. Now, something even more impressive happens with the next three planets: They rule one sign and they co-rule another! Does that sound confusing? Maybe a little bit! But you can use your chart to make it as straightforward as possible!

To be more specific, Mars rules Aries in the first house. At the same time, it co-rules Scorpio along with Pluto in the eighth house. Jupiter rules Sagittarius in the ninth house and co-rules Pisces along with Neptune in the twelfth house. Last but not least, Saturn rules Capricorn in the tenth house and co-rules Aquarius with Uranus in the eleventh house. By planning this out, you can have a chart with all the analogies readily available for you to use any time you want to learn something about the universe.

Another thing you need to remember when you read your astrological chart is the longitude and latitude. There are four points in the chart that you should highlight. More particularly, you get the 'IC' in the fourth house. This is short for "Imum Coeli" or "the bottom of the sky." It is also called the "midnight point" and focuses on your roots, as well as your inner self. 'DC' stands for the 'Descendant' and it is positioned in the seventh house. It is the western angle of the horoscope and determines all you need to acquire before you are able to grow and expand your existence.

'AC' is short for 'Ascendant', and it is located in the first house. Also known as the "rising sign", this sign ascends on the eastern horizon and represents everything that you truly are! The AC is essentially your identity, both your appearance and what lies within you and forms your personality. Completing these four angles, you get the 'MC' in the tenth house. This is short for "Medium Coeli", or 'Midheaven.' The MC is located at the highest point of your astrological chart and reflects your personal success. It shows the world your purpose in life and leads you to your higher self.

Besides these fundamental elements in the birth chart, you should also leave some space for extras. You can use a different page or leave a specific place on top of the chart where you can write these additional elements that will help you interpret the celestial world much more efficiently. In this category, you need to include 'Chiron.' It is located between Saturn and Uranus, always moving in an elliptical orbit. In Greek, Chiron means the "Wounded Healer." This is a marvelous asteroid, rather than a planet! It holds special power and it represents those aspects in your life that have always felt more challenging, leaving you wounded in a way.

In these extras, you should definitely include "Black Moon Lilith" as well. This is not an object or a planet, but more of a specific point. What is amazing about Lilith is that it reflects your impulses without any agenda or filter. It is your deepest, rawest, most primitive form of desires, along with the darkest side of yourself that emerges through this point in the astrological chart. Of course, you should also add four more asteroids in these extra elements of your natal chart! These elements are 'Pallas', 'Juno', 'Vesta', and 'Ceres.' Pallas is Goddess Athena in Greek mythology, the Goddess of wisdom and warfare. Juno is the Goddess of marriage and commitment in Roman mythology. Vesta is the Goddess of home and hearth, while Ceres is the representation of motherhood!

Apart from all that, there are two extremely important elements that you must include: The North and South Nodes of the natal chart are points located right opposite each other and reflect the past and the future. Your South Node reflects your past, your karmic journeys, and where you come from. Any wisdom you have accumulated from your past lives is brought here in this world, armoring you for what lies ahead. On the other hand, your North Node reflects your future. It shows you your true destiny, your calling in this life. This concludes the basic table of your astrological chart and its representation.

After having completed that, it is time to dive even deeper to the planetary powers. What you will focus on is the 'detriment', the 'exaltation', and the 'fall.' These are the fundamental dignities of each planet. The detriment is the planet that is located exactly opposite to the sign it rules. In this case, the planet does not hold abundant strength over the specific sign. On the other hand, exaltation means that the specific sign does hold a strong position and impacts the planet. So, this means that the planet is most suitably positioned at that point. The planet's fall, of course, represents its least powerful position.

Sun rules Leo, but the sign opposite Leo is Aquarius. So the Sun is in detriment in the sign of Aquarius. Respectively, the Moon is in detriment in the sign of Capricorn. When it comes to Mercury, there is Sagittarius. Venus is in detriment in Scorpio, Mars in Libra, Jupiter in Gemini, Saturn in

Cancer, Uranus in Leo, Neptune in Virgo, and finally Pluto in Taurus.

Next step is for you to write down the exaltation and fall options of each planet in your chart. Sun is exalted in the sign of Aries and then falls in the sign of Libra. The Moon is exalted in Taurus and falls in Scorpio. Mercury is exalted in Virgo and falls in Pisces, whereas Venus is exalted in Pisces and falls in Virgo. Mars is exalted in Capricorn and falls in Cancer, while Jupiter is the exact opposite. Saturn is exalted in Libra and falls in Aries, Uranus is exalted in Scorpio and falls in Taurus. Neptune is exalted in Sagittarius and falls in Gemini and, lastly, Pluto is exalted in Leo and falls in Aquarius.

Another wonderful table that you should create (after all that!) is a table that features the elements, the modes, and trinities of the planets. This will also help you interpret your natal chart, which is awesome! As you know, there are four elements and each sign is characterized by a single element. Aries, Leo, and Sagittarius are in the element of fire. Taurus, Virgo, and Capricorn are in the element of earth. Gemini, Libra, and Aquarius are in the element of Air, while finally Cancer, Scorpio, and Pisces are in the element of water.

Regarding modes or modalities, Aries is cardinal, Leo is fixed, and Sagittarius is mutable. For earth signs, Taurus is fixed, Virgo is mutable, and Capricorn is cardinal. Next, Gemini is mutable, Libra is cardinal, and Aquarius is fixed. Lastly, in regards to the water signs, Cancer is cardinal, Scorpio is fixed, and Pisces is mutable. For the next phase, the trinities should be explained further. Aries is ruled by the first house and this is an angular house, representing action. The same goes for the tenth house, ruled by Capricorn, the seventh house ruled by Libra, and the fourth house ruled by Cancer.

In a similar pattern, we have Leo ruled by the fifth house,

which is a succedent house. This means that it is all about sustainment. The same happens with Taurus, ruled by the second house, Aquarius, ruled by the eleventh house and Scorpio, ruled by the eighth house. Cadent trinities are Sagittarius. ruled by the ninth house, Virgo, ruled by the sixth house, Gemini, ruled by the third house, and Pisces, ruled by the twelfth house.

In your natal chart, observe the outer wheel with the signs, and the inner wheel with the planets. When you lay out all the tables that you have prepared so far, you will be able to read your birth chart very accurately. If you are having difficulty in remembering how this works, think of an analogy that works for you. For example, the planets are the actors in a theatrical play, while the signs represent their characters, and the houses compose the actual scene on which the actors perform.

A Brief Guide to Astrological Houses and Signs

The first house is about who you are, and it is ruled by Aries, since the ruling planet is Mars. It is relevant to the way you look and aligns with your physical appearance. Everyone notices it, so it is what we project to the world! It is also a reflection of your childhood experiences. How did you grow up and how did you start interacting with others in the world? All that non-verbal communication is reflected in the first house, and essentially this is the place of your higher self. Moving on to the second house, this is ruled by Taurus and its ruling planet is Venus. It is all about creating! You are building a life for yourself, and therefore Taurus is associated with how you feel about *you*. It depicts your self-esteem and confidence, your self-worth and moral code.

Gemini is the sign of the third house, ruled by Mercury, and it refers to communication on all levels. This house is associated with your siblings, friends, and family, as well as any other person you interact with in your life. It refers to your everyday life and defines how you behave on several occasions. Apart from that, it is the house of intellect, and offers you the chance to adapt to various situations. Corresponding with the energy of Cancer, the fourth house is ruled by Uranus and symbolizes family, along with intimate relationships.

The fifth house is ruled by Leo and the Sun, allowing you to show your creativity to the world! It shows your personal style and how you explore your uniqueness. Your sense of romance and love is also determined by the fifth house, while your relationships with children and how you get along with them is another aspect affected by this particular house. Next is the sixth house, and this is ruled by Virgo. This house corresponds to the energy of Mercury, even though some claim that it is Chiron that rules it. Health and wellness are influenced by this house.

Libra rules the seventh house, corresponding to the energy of Venus. This house is quite special, as it offers you a glimpse at your direct relationships. Are you leaning towards others or are you running away from them? How do you cope with intimacy and feeling close to other people? Is this something that you enjoy, or is it something that you dread? You can see that it is the exact opposite of the first house, which is pretty interesting! Moving on to the eighth house, this is often referred to as the 'haunted house.' It might sound intimidating, but this house relates to sex, death, and the occult, as well as changes of all sorts. As you may have guessed, the eighth house is ruled by Pluto and Scorpio.

The ninth house is ruled by Jupiter and Sagittarius. It has to do with exploration and a constant eagerness to find out more about the world. You may engage in philosophical quests through this house and you may find yourself in an attempt to discover what lies beyond your grasp. You become curious, wiser, and you feel a deep need to travel, to indulge in new experiences. On the other hand, the tenth house is ruled by Capricorn and Saturn. It lies opposite to Cancer, representing a fatherly figure. This house governs your image and the way you appear to others around you. It signifies your success and drives your ambitions.

Before reaching the end, the eleventh house is ruled by Aquarius and Uranus. Linked to your humanitarian pursuits, this is also the house that deals with karmic relationships and alliances that are formed in life. You will also see that it is closely associated with revolutionary concepts and ideas. Finally, the twelfth house is ruled by the energy of Pisces and Neptune. People often call this the "unseen house." This house has to do with things that you cannot see, yet you can feel and understand. It is about the unconscious and escapism. Consequently, this is the house linked to spirituality and intuition.

As soon as you fully comprehend the exact patterns in which every sign and planet collaborate with each other, you become more aware of how the universe affects your very existence. The houses are there to show you how each different energy is manifesting on the earth, influencing you and everyone else around you. This is a magical process that unfolds before your eyes, through the power of these celestial objects shining bright and sharing their precious energy with you!

7

BUILDING THE TOWERING ARCHITECTURE THAT IS YOUR DREAM LIFE: MOON LIFE PLANNING MASTERY

U p to this point, you have gained great insights on how the Moon affects your life on so many different levels. Now is the time to start planning your life based on the full moon and the various moon phases! This is how you are going to construct the masterpiece of your existence, exactly the way you have been dreaming of. I know you are excited about it and you cannot wait for all those marvelous things lying ahead! So, let's focus on the more practical side of Moon interpretation.

As the Moon revolves around the Earth, it influences our planet significantly. Of course, this influence is not the same during the lunar cycle. As I have pointed out earlier in this book, there are many factors taking a toll on the Moon's influence. This is why it is of the essence to truly comprehend when is the time to sit still and recover, as well as when is the perfect time to set your intentions and watch them turn into reality.

I hope that you have been paying attention so far, because the Moon has got so much to offer! Indeed, it is fascinating to see the great impact the Moon can have in your life. It is especially important to know when to focus on actions and when to lay back and remain idle if you are going to make the most out of your lunar experience. So choose your battles wisely!

At the beginning of the lunar cycle, you have no energy. You need to recover and regain your strength in order to pursue your goals a little later. So this is not the time to claim what is rightfully yours, as you will be laboring with no result, and your efforts will be in vain. However, you can always ponder and dream about what you wish to manifest! Slowly, you will be able to start making plans and setting your intentions. Just before the first quarter of the Moon, you will see that your energy is gradually piling up.

Upon entering the waxing gibbous, you have begun to regain your powers and now it is time to take action. What can you do to ensure that your intentions do not go unnoticed? How can you make use of your powers, in order to refine and nurture those goals? This is a greatly beneficial period that can actually influence your life through the energy of the Moon. You are driven by a higher power, an eternal force flowing within you. Have faith in the process and trust the Moon to receive what you want in life.

With the full moon, you should be celebrating. reflecting on what you have wished to receive. The Sun and the Moon have aligned fully, allowing you to praise their magnitude and appreciate the wonders of nature. Prepare yourself to receive gracefully, giving thanks to the universe for everything that you have already received in your life. Feel the mystical aura of the full moon surrounding you, feeling complete and accomplished.

The waning gibbous moon phase is perfect to receive and be grateful. Share those blessings with the world, staying true to your higher self. Find your calling in life and stick with it, before reflecting as the third quarter phase arrives. If your intentions have not been transformed into reality, think about it. What has gone wrong? What could you have done differently? Learn from your experiences and get ready to try again in a little while. For now, in the waning crescent phase, you are encouraged to take it down a notch. Rest, release all the tension that has accumulated thus far, and sigh with relief.

You have made it to the end of yet another lunar cycle. Enjoy stillness, take a deep breath, and let's begin one more cycle around the Earth! A timeless journey that affects us all deserves to be celebrated every single time, because every cycle is unique and holds so many wonderful treasures within! Just reach out and be open to receive them.

A LOOK AT THE DAILY MOON

Every single lunar cycle represents a full journey towards growth. By taking a look at the daily Moon, you can align your life in a way that makes the most out of this powerful celestial element! However, you must first understand how each lunar cycle works. From what you saw earlier, there is a time to sit still and rest in the new moon. Then, there is a time to set intentions and take actions. Right after that, the time comes when you celebrate and be open to receive your blessings. There is a time to reflect and possibly identify any wrongdoings or obstacles standing in the way.

Another factor that you should take into consideration when interpreting the Moon cycle is the zodiac sign on which the Moon falls. This special detail allows you to fully align with the universe and promote your personal growth in the world. According to the specific zodiac sign that affects each lunar cycle, you can adjust your life and ensure that you maximize your odds of achieving your goals, ultimately reaching success. Feel free to explore the lunar cycles of each zodiac sign and understand how they influence you personally.

Aries drives your will to succeed and therefore sparks your passion. During the new moon, Aries allows you to start fresh and identify any challenges that may come along the way. In the waxing moon, this is the sign that drives you to push forward, and keeps motivating you throughout the lunar cycle. During the full moon, it is time for you to take charge of your life and Aries will make sure you do! As the waning moon arrives, Aries will enable you to reclaim your power and adjust your course to make the most of your efforts.

On the other hand, Taurus offers you the opportunity to slow down a little! In the new moon, you will be motivated to appreciate the present and its pleasurable moments. Even if you have not been mindful of your blessings, Taurus will help you. In the waxing moon, Taurus will see that you lay strong foundations for the life you deserve and anticipate. The full moon is the perfect time to celebrate your accomplishments and take the action required to achieve your goals. Abundance and gratitude are prevalent during the waning moon.

Gemini is outgoing and adventurous as a sign. If you are eager to communicate with the universe, then this is a great time to do so... especially during the new moon! In the waxing moon, you prepare yourself for whatever it takes in order to realize your dreams and manifestations. During the full moon, you will be able to ask questions and seek the answers that will assist in your goal-setting. Finally, as the Moon enters the waning period, you will be encouraged to evaluate your course so far.

The sign of Cancer is emotional and vulnerable, focusing on your inner self. In the new moon, Cancer invites you to introspect and identify any emotional issues that have been holding you back from achieving your goals. During the waxing period of the lunar cycle, you should modify your actions as per the realization of your emotional triggers. The full moon is a great time for you to embrace your emotional vulnerability, rather than shying away from emotions altogether! Lastly, you will see how these emotions actually affect you in the waning moon.

You already know that Leo is daring and brave! In the new moon, Leo will urge you to face your fears and reflect on their meaning. During the waxing period, you will be asked to conquer those fears. You should realize why they have such an effect on you before you can take action and crush them. Under the full moon, Leo will guide you towards seeing your truth and letting go of your hesitations. In the waning period, you will be ready to take pleasure from your life as it is and boost your confidence!

Moving on to the sign of Virgo: This is definitely the time to organize things and keep them neat and tidy. In the new moon, you will be driven to form new habits that benefit you in the long run. Your mind will shift in a positive way that allows you to be happy and accomplish your goals. During the waxing moon, you must focus on understanding whether or not your routines are good for you. In the full moon, Virgo will enable you to reflect on your current situation and see if this is what truly makes you happy. Finally, the waning period brings clarity in your life and offers you a glimpse at the wider picture.

Libra is the sign of balance and alignment. The new moon in Libra offers you a chance to understand if something has fallen out of balance. If so, what can you do to remedy the situation? Even if you can't do that just yet, you should try to let your displeasure go. It may be time to change your perspective and this is what the waxing period allows you to do! In the full moon, you fully comprehend what messes with your alignment and you prepare yourself to let go. As the Moon continues its course and you enter the waning period, you should listen to your heart and let it take the lead.

Mystery and change define Scorpio, which is the sign that allows you to take a good look deep within you. In the full moon, set your intentions to truly understand who you are and what you enjoy. Understand your passions and deepest desires, so that you start pursuing them during the waxing moon. As the full moon approaches, it is time to set out on your path towards bringing those passions and desires into your life. Finally, the waning period is the time for you to interpret your behavior and see why you do things the way you do.

If you wish to flourish, Sagittarius will lead the way. The new moon in Sagittarius enables you to step forward and claim the life that you deserve! Discover what makes your heart beat faster and set the intentions of receiving those blessings. In the waxing moon, you should identify the obstacles that hinder your happiness and make sure you take action. The full moon is the time to focus on your truth, releasing any negativity and past experiences that have dragged you down. Last but not least, the waning period is when you come to terms with your emotional self.

Unlike Sagittarius, Capricorn will bring you back to Earth. In the new moon, you will be motivated to set more realistic intentions that are aligned with yourself. What is your true calling and what do you need to succeed in your life's purpose? The waxing moon is the time to make necessary changes, in order to accomplish your goals. Get real in the full moon, with Capricorn awakening you and pushing you towards self-realization. Be efficient and see those goals turn into reality during the waning period.

Focus on you and you alone when the new moon is in Aquarius. A free spirit, Aquarius guides you to discover who you really are. Choose to be independent and work towards self-accomplishment throughout the waxing period of the moon. Under the full moon, you can communicate with your deepest self and bring to surface your desires. Express yourself, do not hold back, and do not postpone getting what you want. In the waning period, this is exactly what you should focus on!

Wrapping up the zodiac signs, Pisces is all about ethereal spirituality. In the new moon, set your intentions regarding your spiritual self and focus on your transformation. During the waxing period, you will be able to explore your strengths and weaknesses, becoming wiser in the process. The full moon brings awareness to your emotional state and allows you to see why you really feel that way. Finally, the waning period lets all the sunshine in and brings clarity into your soul, as you truly see who you are meant to be in this life!

How to Start a Moon Journal for Personal Growth

Visual representations are always great assets when it comes to focusing on different aspects of your existence and your connection to the world. This is why it is so crucial to keep a moon journal, as you can truly delve into the mysteries of lunar cycles and explore their effects on your life. Are you looking forward to transforming your existence and welcoming enlightenment? Then you need a pen or pencil, colorful markers, a cute journal that speaks into your soul, and, of course, a positive attitude!

What you need to do first is to draw the lunar cycle in as much detail as possible. You can find templates online, so you can print them out and glue them into your journal. The printables should show you the moon phases (new moon, waxing moon, full moon, waning moon etc.) and have them as a reference. They all form a cycle, starting with stillness, moving all the way into action, and then flowing down again. In this way, through this visualization, you will realize how the energy flows, and how all these phases are interconnected.

With every lunar cycle, you should concentrate on setting new intentions. Once again, you can plan ahead based on the zodiac sign where the Moon falls every month. For instance, if you wish to set spiritual intentions, then Pisces Moon is the perfect time to do that! Use your creativity in your journal for each particular lunar cycle. You can draw pictures or print them online, or even use old scrapbooks and magazines. Whatever makes you feel happy and works for you is great here, as you create this themed cycle with the moon phases for yourself only. Give that cycle a name and then create a diary.

It is equally important to keep a journal of your actions throughout the specific lunar cycle. You can turn the page and make room for a detailed monthly diary, where each day you add everything you have done towards realizing your goals. This will be your monthly challenge! Again, draw and fill it out in a way that motivates you to come back to the journal. In this diary, you can also add how you feel and describe your mood. As a result, you may see what effects the Moon has on you! It will help you better understand yourself.

It is also advised that you keep a special weekly spread with your actions and anything else you wish to reflect on more carefully. On a different page you can focus on each moon phase and analyze what this is all about. In the new moon, you will concentrate on setting your new intentions, while in the waxing period you will take action. Write down your specific objectives for this exact week and monitor your progress. This is going to be tangible proof of whether or not you have accomplished your goals. Furthermore, tracking what happens in your life can serve as a way to identify the barriers that have prevented you from reaching your goals.

Be consistent with your moon journal and you will be able to fully comprehend yourself, shedding light to those parts that you have not even realized are there! By tracking your mood, your actions, and the boundaries that keep you from enjoying what you want, you will have the opportunity to modify your behavior and reach happiness! If you are determined to achieve personal growth and use the eternal power of the Moon to guide you in your path, then you should make a habit of creating a moon journal and staying true to it. After a few lunar cycles, its impact is going to be astonishing!

8

BATHE IN THE MOON'S ENERGY TO CLEANSE WHAT NO LONGER SERVES YOU

T he Moon is magical, offering its healing properties to you. Immerse yourself in its powerful energy and get in full alignment with the universe. Once you start living in harmony with nature and its mysteries, you will see that everything comes together. Build a strong bond and heal yourself, letting go of whatever no longer serves your life purpose.

Even if you have been hurt before, the new moon represents new beginnings. Start fresh and delve into the Moon's power. This is another motivation for you to pursue happiness, self-accomplishment, and success through your actions. Plant the seeds that you wish to grow in your garden, wishing on the Moon for prosperity and successful outcomes. It is a time of rebirth, rejuvenation, and absolute dedication to your cause! Do not let anything poison your soul, keeping you away from what you can achieve in life.

There are many ways for you to embrace and harness the lunar energy. Bathe under the moonlight to feel its power flowing right through you. Light a candle and reflect on the moon phases, feeling what they represent every single night. Gaze up at the sky, observing the Moon and its exact position. The Moon is able to see your soul, so feel free to open up and receive its blessings! Visualize your goals and feel totally relaxed, trusting in the Moon for accomplishing them in the end. Even if it takes a while, the entire experience is worth it!

Connect yourself to the Moon, creating an everlasting bond that is hard to break. Embrace your spirituality and allow the Moon to guide you. Your inner child is trapped in isolation, and through this powerful connection you can let go of past traumas, enabling your inner child to finally breathe and become liberated. The Moon represents your feminine divine energy, your intuition, and your psychic abilities. Therefore, being connected to it means that you accept your spiritual self and achieve a holistic balance in your life.

The Moon is so powerful and it cleanses all negativity from your life! If you allow it to flow through you, the Moon will get rid of anything toxic and help you elevate your vibrational frequencies. It will assist you on your path towards healing your deeper self. No matter how painful the process might be, in the end you are going to be reborn. You will be stronger than ever, more confident in your own powers, and fully aligned with the universe.

HEALING YOURSELF WITH THE ENERGY OF THE MOON

Your body is your temple, and you must think of it as a sacred vessel. Many people forget just how important it is to keep their body in a pristine state, seeking health and rejecting anything that might hinder their progress. Be in tune with the lunar cycle, modifying your actions accordingly to reach the highest levels of spiritual awareness. Learn when is the time to rest, recover, heal, and introspect. Then, get ready to fuel your passion, take necessary action, and nurture your goals, ensuring that you meet them by the end of the cycle.

During the waning period, as the Moon goes into darkness, you should take a break to focus on your health. This is the time to relax, clearing your chakras and cleansing your aura. Get rid of toxicity in your life, sigh with relief, and engage in meditation for optimal results in communicating with your inner self. Deep breathing will help you dispose of anxiety and in turn, listen to what your body is telling you. Be conscious and set your intentions mindfully. In the waxing period, you should focus on energizing your body, taking the steps required to reach your goals. Let the positive energy of the Moon flow right through you, elevating your frequency, and therefore welcoming all those glorious intentions into your reality.

Below you will find a full moon ritual that can help you heal with the power of the Moon! Use that to concentrate on positive vibes and let go of the barriers that mess with your balance. Furthermore, it is beneficial to take moon baths by observing the Moon during the lunar cycle, and letting its glow shine through you. Be open to receiving its energy, welcoming it into your life, and feeling the Moon as it blesses you with its special powers! Engage in power charged meditations that enable you to delve deeper and align with the cosmos. The world is your oyster if you simply understand how it works!

During the full moon, a great way to supercharge your life is to dance under the moonlight! Let go of your worries and feel like a child again! This is your time to enjoy, relish those moments of innocence and dance exactly the way you feel like it. No one is there to judge you or make you feel uncomfortable. So start swaying and dancing to the beat of your favorite music or simply follow your inner rhythm. It is a therapeutic method to release negative energy and let go of your emotional baggage. On the other hand, you should understand your limitations during this point of the lunar cycle. Do not make any sudden decisions based on an impulse, as the full moon tends to heighten all emotions and create more drama. Instead, take some time to distance yourself from any situation and relax.

Embrace harmony from within, listening to your body throughout each lunar cycle. Feel its positive effects on you both physically and mentally. This is an ongoing journey towards self-growth and expansion! You should always be grateful for what you have already received in your life, praising the universe for the abundance you enjoy. Allow your body to heal naturally, without putting any pressure on it. Instead, cleanse your chakras to create a channel connecting you to the Earth and the sky above. Receive the nurturing properties of the Moon and watch the magic unfold.

Leave Space for Miracles to Happen

Everything in life happens for a reason. As we are part of the universe, we are divine! Therefore, we are responsible for all the blessings that we receive. All the miracles that we seek in the world are essentially our making. It is up to us to see the silver lining in every single misstep or difficult experience. Even in the darkest of times, we should learn valuable lessons from those negative things that happen. We must accept them and forgive them. Only in this way can we remain calm and let go of the negativity, so that the true miracles can eventually brighten our life. And this cannot happen without cleansing and creating the space for those miracles.

You should take the initiative and cleanse your life of everything bad that has been holding you back! I am going to show you how to get rid of those toxic thoughts and harmful patterns in your life, how to release the lower energies and make room for high frequencies. The full moon is the perfect timing for you to forgive and heal, as this is when your emotions are heightened and you become most spiritually aware. You should therefore carry out a full moon ritual to cleanse from everything negative, and make space for all the wonderful things that you are about to receive.

First of all, create a sacred space. I have referred to this earlier in the book. Cleanse the atmosphere from negative auras and invite new, positive auras instead in a place you feel safe. You can burn sage for a thorough cleansing of the atmosphere, Palo Santo sticks, or even scented candles and incense. Then, start writing down on a piece of paper all the things you wish to let go of. You can write a list, always beginning with the words, *I release...* and then continue on to name everything you wish to release. This is spiritual purging for you, so you can expect being emotional throughout the ritual.

Be gentle, in order to be the best version of your life. As you are writing down your list, you will realize that you feel like a huge burden has been lifted off your chest. Gradually, you will start feeling happier and this means that you no longer hold any grudges, or any anger towards those things you release. At the end of the list, you should conclude with the following statement: *I demand that all bodies, thoughts, vibrations, frequencies, and patterns that are anchoring the energy I wish to release, actually leave me and my energy. I demand that they leave me on all layers of existence, beyond dimensions and time. You do not belong here with me. I declare that this is the truth, according to my highest self and the greatest good.*

Be present in the moment and read through your list out loud, concluding with your statement. After doing that, it is now time to burn the paper! Use a tray or a pot to avoid any accidents. Pick up a candle or a lighter and burn the paper, as the physical representation of this release. Watch the paper burn and feel the beneficial effects of this ritual within your soul. Pick up the ashes and dispose of them safely. Take a deep breath and sigh with relief. By completing this ritual, you have made it clear that you are open to receive the miracles you are looking forward to. So, now it is up to the universe to grant you what you have requested!

❧ 9 ❧

THE NEXT LEVEL: MOON MAGIC
MASTERY

I am positive that you are already feeling the magnitude of the Moon energy in your life. It is a thrilling experience and I could not be happier for you! Now it is time to learn how to master Moon magic and optimize your success in every single lunar cycle. Once you understand how to harness the energy of the Moon, you will be blessed with an eternal gift of fully aligning with nature, and can receive its blessings without anything holding you back.

One of the biggest steps for you to take towards utilizing the celestial elements to your advantage is to create a spiritual altar. I know that it might sound impossible to have a dedicated place to call your own, without anyone touching it. Especially if you live with a bunch of other people. When part of a large family, for example, privacy tends to be underrated or even ignored completely. However, this is crucial to your future as a glorious witch that wants to conquer nature through spells, rituals, meditation, and so much more.

If you are having trouble deciding where to place your altar, then you need to close your eyes and understand where it feels right. It can be in your bedroom, in the backyard, in the living room, or anywhere else. Moreover, it doesn't matter how much space it takes! You are free to decide, as long as it makes you feel comfortable and safe. In order to enhance safety, you should include a white and a red candle in your altar. Black salt in a cute little jar is also great, as well as pyrite crystal. It is important that you light your candles on a daily basis, or at least when you meditate.

From that point, you can use your imagination to add some character in your altar. Other crystals and incense, scented candles and flowers, plants and small decorative statuettes, your journal or other books that inspire you, can all be used to maximize the spiritual power of your altar. You can also include pictures of your loved ones or your ancestors, as they are guiding your spirit. If you practice tarot readings, then keep the tarot oracle cards close by, along with a comfortable cushion. Anything that makes you feel at home is great to add in your personal sacred place.

When you are at your altar, nothing can harm you! The time you spend there is absolutely magical, so make sure that you nurture this feeling of safety and protection. Practice your spells and rituals, meditate and engage in deep breathing exercises, write in your journal, and of course indulge in chakra cleansing. You can also manifest what you wish to receive in life, express your gratitude, and perform any ritual you believe helps you in your spiritual path.

MEDITATIONS AND RITUALS FOR THE FULL MOON

The full moon can feel so electric, since all energies are on high alert. As a result, magic is most potent during this time of the lunar cycle. Those 72 hours around the full moon are the best for you to practice any full moon ritual or meditation, maximizing their effectiveness. It is entirely up to you how you are going to take advantage of these magnificent hours when the full moon illuminates you in its healing powers.

There are many different things that you can do during the full moon. It doesn't have to be anything fancy. You can simply gather your crystals and go outside on your porch (or maybe by the beach), basking under the full moon and bathing in its glorious healing light. Give thanks to the full moon and connect on a deeper level, honoring its very core. Show your loving gratitude to the Moon for every single blessing that has come into your life. This is a great and simple, yet extremely powerful, way to express your appreciation.

If you are determined to conduct a full moon ritual, you must first check the zodiac sign to see which astrological sign the Moon is under. After identifying the exact properties of the specific full moon, you will be able to adjust your ritual for optimal results. In this way, you will be working with the particular energies surrounding the atmosphere instead of deciding on impulse what to manifest. That being said, you can still manifest whatever you want! A tarot reading is another wonderful asset in your hands, so you can call in any deities you feel might enhance your ritual.

Prior to the ritual itself, you should focus on meditation. Take deep breaths and listen to some relaxing music which inspires you and allows you to transcend into the universe. Concentrate and be present in the moment, while casting a circle and creating the sacred space for you to proceed with your ritual. You can use any scented candles, add your crystals, and use any other item that you think will help you meditate. As you are grounding yourself, you also need to be aware of the specific elements you are going to bring into the ritual. If the Moon falls under a water sign, then water should be prevalent during the ritual.

The witching hour is ideal for you to perform your ritual. This is of course around midnight, when the energy is at its peak! What you need to do is define what your heart truly desires and manifest it under the full moon. The secret lies within asking with a pure heart. Visualize the energy of the Moon beaming down on you. Then, imagine that you are holding that pure silvery light into your palms and you are channeling it into whatever you wish to manifest.

A wonderful way for you to shower yourself with the energy of the Moon is to purify your sacral chakra and channel the moonlight through that, causing your entire body to be overwhelmed by this magnificent beam of light. Keep in mind that magic is your innate nature, so this should come naturally to you. Be mindful of the spells you are casting and the energy that you are releasing. According to what you wish to achieve, it would be advisable not to perform those rituals exactly on the full moon. On the contrary, you may find it more beneficial to conduct these rituals and cleansing procedures a day earlier or later than the full moon.

When there are eclipses taking place during a specific lunar cycle, you are especially advised to wait it out and perform your rituals later. Otherwise, you would be risking that energy backfiring on you. After all, nature might interpret your rituals as a means of manipulation and this is never a good thing. Even if you have the nicest intentions, you must be patient and enjoy the full moon without manifesting anything on that particular night. The energy will be high even on the next night for you to benefit from through your rituals.

Insights on Different Moons & Eclipses

There are several terms that might baffle you when trying to interpret the lunar cycle. I am going to explain some of these terms, so that you can fully comprehend what they mean, and understand the universe even more profoundly. First of all, I am sure you have heard that Mercury is in retrograde, and that this can affect people on many levels. The truth is that Mercury does not change its course and does not move backwards. However, it appears to do so!

The reason behind this phenomenon is the distance between Mercury and the Sun. Since this is in fact the closest planet when it comes to the Sun, its orbit is much smaller. As a result, it seems that at a specific point it slows down a little and the Earth is able to pass by. This is when it appears to be moving in retrograde. Although this is an illusion, you still need to remember that this phenomenon brings turbulence to the cosmos. So do not make any final decisions and do not choose to do anything radical then.

Eclipses happen when the Sun, the Moon, and the Earth align with each other. A total eclipse of the Moon is called a "Red Moon" or a "Blood Moon." This happens when the Moon travels through the Earth's 'umbra', which is basically the center of its shadow. As a result, the Sun does not illuminate the Moon directly. On the contrary, the light is reflected on the Earth and then illuminates the Moon. So the Moon appears to be a reddish color, although sometimes the color can range from orange to dark yellow.

This can be an emotionally challenging time, with the Red Moon affecting people's sleep patterns and overall mood. As mentioned above, the umbra is the inner part of a shadow. The Earth's umbra causes the lunar eclipses, which can either be partial or full. 'Penumbra', on the other hand, is the lighter part of the shadow. Finally, there is also the 'antumbra.' This is the external rim of the shadow that is visible beyond the umbra. It is especially evident during the annular eclipse, which takes place when the Moon's surface covers the Sun entirely, creating a fiery ring all around.

Moving on to the "Blue Moon", this is yet another spectacular phenomenon up in the sky! Although there are several occasions when the Moon does appear blue, in fact a Blue Moon simply means the second full moon within a single calendar month. It is a rather rare phenomenon, taking place approximately every 30 months! If you are wondering why, then you should take into account that a lunar cycle lasts around 29.5 days. However, months have 30 or 31 days. So, this leaves room for the Blue Moon to occur.

If you are interested in learning what a "Flower Moon" is, you will be happy to know that it is the full moon in May, which is compared to a flower that slowly blooms in spring. In January, we have the "Wolf Moon." February is the time for the "Snow Moon", March is when the "Worm Moon" occurs, and April is great for the "Pink Moon." After May, in June we have the "Strawberry Moon", and then July is when the "Buck Moon" occurs. A "Sturgeon Moon" is in August, "Harvest Moon" in September or October, divided into a full "Corn Moon" or "Hunter's Moon." To complete the monthly full moon calendar, November is the "Beaver Moon" and December is the "Cold Moon."

POWER CHARGED MOON CYCLE
AND NEW MOON ASTROLOGY
GUIDED MEDITATIONS

There is no better time in the lunar cycle than the new moon for you to manifest what you wish to receive in life. As a result, you should make sure that you supercharge your spirituality and establish a deep connection with the Moon, as one more lunar cycle begins. This is a key element if you want to take advantage of the glorious power of the Moon towards projecting your dreams and desires into reality.

Once again, you can always combine these meditations with tarot readings! Depending on the exact phase of the Moon, your readings can enlighten you on so many different things. For instance, the new moon is a great time to use your tarot oracle readings for new things, while the waxing moon period is perfect for things you already have in your life. The full moon is all about intuition, whereas the waning period is ideal for eliminating things from your life. Work around these moon phases and watch these mysteries unfold before your eyes!

Below I have gathered some of the most effective, power-ful, magical meditations for you to try out during the new moon. As you can see, they focus on different aspects of the very same thing. This is the time for new beginnings, the time to let go of the past and move forward. Set new intentions, take action to bring them into your life, and become aware of the blockages that hinder your progress. Heal, recover, rise from the ashes, and claim what is rightfully yours, always with the help of the omnipresent Moon.

GUIDED MEDITATION TO MANIFEST YOUR DREAMS

What would you like to bring into your life? Through this guided meditation, you will be able to manifest all those marvelous things, and enjoy the benefits of the new moon towards supercharging your new intentions.

For this meditation, sit somewhere comfortably. Find your spiritual altar and place your palms on your lap. Close your eyes and focus on your breathing. As you are breathing in through your nose, feel your lungs filling with fresh air. Breathe out through your mouth, emptying your lungs until you feel your belly button lift. Repeat the same pattern of deep breaths in order for your body to relax and become lighter.

Visualize just one thing that you would like to welcome into your life. Focus on this thought, trying to analyze why you want that. Why of all things have you chosen to bring this into your life? What will it offer you? How will it affect your everyday life and what impact will it have on your spiritual journey? What kind of feelings will it spark? You do not need to think of the way you are going to bring this into your life, as you must have faith in the process. Feel those emotions of positivity, pleasure, love, security, everything that is associated with bringing this specific thing into your life.

Repeat to yourself: *I manifest what is best for the good of all.*

Keep your eyes closed. You can repeat this as many times as you like so that you become absolutely certain that you are going to actually acquire it at the end of this cycle. When you are ready to regain full consciousness, do so without letting go of your certainty. Whatever it is you have manifested will indeed flourish and be brought into your reality. You trust the process and have no doubts about it. What you have manifested is already yours!

Now let go, allowing the universe to work its magic. Remember to take deep breaths. Breathe in through your nose. Open your mouth and let all the air out completely. Repeat the same process twice again, so as to release any tension that has piled up. Feel utterly relaxed, as you begin to stretch your hands above your head. Press your palms together right above your head, and then move them down until you reach your heart and chest.

Remember, *what you think you become, what you feel you attract, what you imagine you create*, and be grateful for the experience. Give thanks to the universe for granting your desires and manifesting that special thing you have attracted into your life. I am sure that by now a huge smile has lit up your face! You feel that sense of accomplishment overwhelming you! It is that exceptional feeling of fullness you are experiencing. Take a few moments to enjoy this feeling and then get on with your day, always keeping in mind the magnificent experience you had.

GUIDED MEDITATION TO CLEAR FINANCIAL BLOCKS & ATTRACT MONEY

Who doesn't want some extra money, especially if it is completely out of the blue? Through this guided meditation, you will get the chance to clear any negativity that results in financial blocks, making room for more money coming your way!

Close your eyes and relax, relaxing your body. Breathe in and out deeply, slowly, focusing on nothing but your breath. Feel safe in the present moment. Release the tension and pressure in every single muscle of your body, letting go of all burdens. With every breath, you relax even more and you delve deeper into your creative mind. Now travel away, visualizing that you are in a verdant forest with the Sun rays shining down on you gracefully.

As the Sun showers you with its golden light, repeat: *I am worthy of financial abundance and love. I am richly rewarded for everything I give to the world. I am fully supported, protected, and deeply loved. Prosperity comes into my life effortlessly. Money is good and I know that. Money is easy and it flows to me with great ease. I feel such a deep sense of peace.* Through the Law of Attraction, everything you want comes easily to you.

Soak in this wonderful experience, observing the peaceful landscape and noticing even the slightest detail. Listen to the leaves gently flowing with the autumn breeze, while smelling the delightful aromas of nature. Think, *I am in alignment with the source of all creation. Everything I need is already here for me. My life is perfectly synchronized. I am in tune with my higher self and the world around me. The universe is taking care of everything I need.* As you are observing closer, you allow yourself to be enveloped in pure luxury.

Continue your positive affirmations, so that you visualize those marvelous images and clear your sacral chakra. Think, *I attract great and wonderful experiences. I bathe in unpretentious prosperity. I deserve the best and I accept it now with open arms. Furthermore, I receive with ease everything I want in my life, all that my heart desires.* Slowly, the Sun goes down to sleep and the Moon takes its place with its healing silvery light. Remember to be thankful: *Thank you for my endless abundance, thank you universe for my wealth. Thank you for bringing me unlimited money. I have planted the seed in my subconscious mind and now I am already reaping the fruit of my manifestations.*

Finally, feel gratitude overwhelming you for all that you have received so far. All this money, all this abundance in your life is brought to you by the universe: *I am filled with gratitude and aligned with the universe, allowing this energy constantly coming my way and bringing me wealth beyond limits. Thank you.* When you are done, slowly open your eyes and feel that lovely sense of abundance flowing through you. You are fully aware of what the universe has granted you, so you feel at peace with the world and enjoy life to its fullest potential!

GUIDED MEDITATION FOR INNER HEALING

Do you wish to prepare yourself for something new in your life? Do you feel wounded by the past? This guided meditation will allow you to let go of the past, heal your inner self, and recharge your spiritual energy, getting ready for a glorious future ahead.

Tend to your spiritual altar and sit comfortably, closing your eyes and concentrating on deep breathing. Let your breath flow easily, effortlessly, like a summer breeze gently rocking the boats at the seashore. Clear your mind and open your heart to receive the light energy that is all around you. Visualize the sky with millions of stars scattered all around and shining down on you eternally. Imagine the new moon that you cannot see, but you can feel through its energy that connects you to the entire universe.

Receive the healing properties of the new moon, as you are blessed by its powerful energy. The new moon is the perfect time to set intentions and create visions. It is also great for clearing your path, letting go of the negativity, and focusing solely on positive new beginnings. What do you wish to create in this new lunar cycle? Bring that into your mind and clear your thoughts. What do you want to receive? What are your goals? Set your intentions deep inside your heart. Watch them grow as the Moon becomes lighter and shines even more beautifully.

Everything that surrounds you contributes to the success of your goals, allowing you to bring them into reality. Imagine how everything supports you in your direction towards fulfilling your goals. Continue looking up in the sky, observing its vastness. Breathe in and out deeply, feeling the new chapter in your life that has already begun. You have turned over a new leaf and the universe supports you fully, unconditionally. Nothing can harm you, as long as you have that vast power by your side! You are refreshed, ready to take on the new challenges in your life.

Your life is moving in the direction of your desire and everything is fully aligned to help you reach your goals. You will grow side by side with the new moon, expanding with each phase, and glowing with the full moon. As the new moon shines brighter every day of the lunar cycle, you will also radiate with light and joy! There is nothing able to bring you down, since you have the support of the divine. You have been blessed with the energy of the new moon and nothing can hinder your progress on this spiritual path you have set out to walk on.

As you have let go of all the toxicity, release yourself from unwanted and harmful habits, as you are now reborn. Breathe deeply and feel the energy of the Moon guiding you in your course. You are not alone. You are healed and you are ready to start afresh. Stay in this feeling for as long as you like. Then open your eyes gently and sigh with relief.

GUIDED MEDITATION WITH THE ANGELS TO BRING ETHERIC ENERGY INTO YOUR LIFE

The angels are powerful beings that can help you replenish your depleted energy and reach the highest levels of vibrational frequencies. Through this guided meditation, you join the wonderful energy of the angels, and become blessed to manifest your fullest potential.

Archangel Michael, Uriel, Gabriel, and Raphael are by your side, connecting with you during this meditation. Create your sacred space and allow the pillars of light from above to wash down on you. Let go of any attachments, body aches, worries. And just for now, let go of attachments to anyone else in your life, and whatever else you have to do today. Let go of the mental body and your thoughts. Tune in to the pure love glowing within you, flowing through you. This is your truth emerging from within you. It is recalibrating you, so that you become open to receive the blessings of divine light into your life.

Channel this light all the way above your head, creating a strong bond and a deep connection between your body and the cosmos above. Communicate with the archangels, as you open yourself and get ready to receive the light transmission to illuminate your consciousness. This is revealing your direct unity with all that is, while also maintaining your individuality. Moving downwards, this golden light is channeled from your crown chakra to your mind and brings heightened awareness and clarity.

Traveling even further down to your throat, this glorious light allows you to speak clearly and purifies this center of energy. Next is your heart, with the light shining brightly and warming it up. Your heart opens and is ready to receive the golden light frequency of awakened solar love, cleansed of all worry and fear. This love allows consciousness to expand and clears your etheric energy, empowering you to shine brighter and vibrate at higher levels.

Allow the same wondrous light to travel even further below to your willpower center, enabling you to act based on your inspiration, in alignment with divine love. Feel empowered and recharged, able to manifest blessings you wish to receive in your life. Now move towards your sacral chakra, purifying this creative center, empowering your truest divine embodiment to anchor down and embody your etheric energy. This will allow your body to remain grounded, blessed by eternal love. Feel that you are safe, supported, and empowered to embody the highest form of love.

Now that your body is purified, your heart is open, you are ready to receive love in its purest form and all the endless possibilities will flow through you. You are blessed by the universe, guided by the archangels. A new beginning is here, now. Reach out and seize the day, opening up to new experiences that help you continue on your spiritual path. Feel the energy surrounding you. You have been blessed and you have received abundance in your life, through the etheric energy of the celestial beings shining down on you. Open your eyes, feel that sensation of completeness, and give thanks to the universe for being so generous.

THE LUNAR MASTERY 30-
MINUTE DAILY RITUAL TO
SKYROCKET YOUR EXISTENCE

B y now you have become a true expert in the power of
the Moon and you have already acquired the knowledge required to optimize its effects on your life.
Below I am going to lay down the most effective rituals that
have worked for me. These rituals will allow you to unlock
your fullest potential, vibrating at the highest levels of
frequencies to transform your entire life.

Unless you change your daily routine and let go of any
past habits that have been dragging you down, you cannot
expect to experience the magnitude of lunar energy. You will
only get to a point and then keep wondering what you are
doing wrong. You must modify your behavior accordingly and
stop hindering the flow of energy into your life. It is time to
get practical and see how your actions can indeed affect your
progress, and either make or break your spiritual
advancement.

As you will see, I have laid out a morning ritual which will
help you boost your day, and project everything you want into
the world. I have also created a special nighttime ritual to
relax, rest, and be fully in tune with the Moon's energy. Feel

free to make the necessary changes that reflect your own, personal preferences. You can add more meditations, rituals, spells, and other ways to find your inner balance.

Remember to be consistent in these rituals, as they will help you find that precious harmony you have been searching for all this time. Do not sabotage yourself by indulging in unhealthy habits that only bring you down and lower your vibrational frequencies. Instead, think smart and incorporate the right habits that allow you to unlock the purest form of lunar energy, welcoming all the blessings you desire in your life.

DAILY RITUAL FORMULA

So let's dive right in, and see how you can start your morning with an easy-to-follow ritual that skyrockets your existence and allows you to supercharge the rest of the day! First of all, make sure that you get enough sleep. I know that several moon phases might mess with your sleep patterns, but do try to relax and get an adequate amount of sleep. Otherwise, the following day you are going to be in a bad mood and you will not have the energy it takes to achieve greatness.

Take a few moments to make your bed and complete the first task of the day as early as possible. This will fill you with pride, as it represents an accomplishment of yours. It doesn't matter how trivial it may seem because it is indeed something you have completed successfully in your daily routine! Then open the windows and let the sunshine in, along with the fresh air and the soothing sounds of the morning. Of course, it would be ideal if you could pop out of your home and enjoy nature. However, even opening the shutters and allowing the new day's glow to bathe your bedroom helps you wake up naturally, and lifts your spirit. Take some deep breaths and appreciate the present moment, observing the sky to see if the Moon is still out there.

Brew some coffee or tea and prepare a healthy breakfast, as this will allow you to be mindful of your morning. Before doing that, it is important that you drink some water. You can make your own Moon water by charging it under the moonlight and drinking it first thing in the morning. In this way, you will be able to absorb the energy of the Moon and bring it with you into your day. Just dedicate a few minutes to enjoying your breakfast, sipping on this liquid bliss in a mug or a tall glass and reflecting on your day. Listen to your favorite music, light a scented candle, and enjoy being present.

As you can understand, the lunar cycle dictates different approaches to your daily ritual. So depending on the exact moon phase, you should then sit comfortably at your spiritual altar and get your journal out. If you are on the new moon, then you must set your intentions. Write down what you want to manifest during this lunar cycle and be as detailed as possible. Later on in the cycle, you can turn back to those intentions and figure out how to act towards accomplishing your goals. Once again, during the full moon, you should celebrate and be thankful. During the waning period, you must focus on releasing the tension and negativity, slowly accepting the ending of yet another lunar cycle.

Spend a few moments with your journal and be creative. You can try drawing or expressing whatever your heart desires on a piece of paper. Reflect on your thoughts and desires, visualizing them and making them part of your reality. If you close your eyes and visualize everything in which you wish to succeed in life, your mood will be lifted even more in an instant. You will be vibrating at higher frequencies, allowing for the Law of Attraction to grant you your wishes. This is a great way to start your day, picturing that you have already received these blessings into your life. While you are visualizing, you can repeat positive affirmations that enhance your experience. For instance, you can say, *I have abundance in my life, I feel blessed and full, my career has skyrocketed and my personal life gives me endless joy.* Even if you do not already have all those things in your life, try to see these things in your mind.

After having completed your visualization, it is time for some supercharging EFT sessions! This is especially important to do in the period right before the new moon, as this clears negativity and makes space for the new intentions you are about to set. Through EFT tapping, you stimulate different parts of your body by tapping your fingers on them to elevate vibration. In this way, you will release the tension and stress that has been piling up, clearing any blockages and allowing your blessings to set in.

You start at the top of your head, using two fingers to tap while repeating the following: *I am worthy. I release whatever no longer serves me. I welcome abundance in my life.* Move down to the center between your eyebrows, while sighing with relief. Continue by tapping the area of your face right below your eyes, repeating those positive affirmations. Of course, you can adjust them according to the exact moon phase to optimize your results and make the most of your intentions. Keep on tapping the upper lip, the chin and then your throat, the chest and under your armpits. After completing a full round, do this again until you feel comforted.

If you want, you can even write down your morning ritual

and stick it on your fridge, or keep it by your bedside table. You can stick it on your wall as a source of inspiration, decorated in a way that sparks joy and speaks right to your heart. Prepare a cute to-do list like the following:

- Create a welcoming atmosphere.
- Make my bed.
- Sip on some Moon water.
- Prepare my morning beverage and breakfast.
- Journal at my altar.
- Visualize my goals.
- Take time for EFT tapping.

This will be your morning guide towards a day filled with endless potential! Obviously, you can tweak this ritual as per your own preferences. Instead of visualization, you can step into a few moments of mindful meditation while listening to inspirational music. You can also add some yoga into the mix, if you wish to stretch and get your energy flowing. Otherwise, you can work out a little indoors or go out for a jog after this ritual is over. Whatever you do, do not put pressure on yourself! Let your moves flow naturally, aligning fully to the universe and surrendering to the energy of the Moon.

One more note before moving on to a wonderful night-time ritual is about crystals. They can be amazing assets when used properly during the lunar cycle, and they can be charged or cleansed under the full moon. During the new moon, you can use black obsidian, labradorite, and black kyanite. The full moon calls for selenite, moonstone, and clear quartz. In between cycles, you can always use black tourmaline, clear quartz, and tourmalinated quartz for optimal results. See which of these crystals serve your purpose, and of course combine them with crystals that match your personality for the optimal results!

Nighttime Ritual

A full day has passed and you have finally returned home. I am sure you are feeling exhausted and the only thing you want is to relax. However, instead of crawling on the sofa and binge-watching a TV series, you can do so much more. You must remember that Moon mastery calls for your actions too! So dedicate some time to yourself, clearing your mind, and letting go of all negativity. I would advise you to shower in the evening, as the healing power of the water will purify your body and mind.

Another thing that allows you to make the most of your evening are Moon salutations, known as "Chandra Namasakar." In this exercise, you give thanks to the Moon and become part of its calming power. It is greatly helpful for you to do these Moon salutations at night, as they are channeling feminine divine energy from the Moon. So right before bed, if you want to embrace the lunar balance in your life, you must perform these yoga poses and fully relax.

First do the mountain pose. As you are standing up with your feet together, open your palms facing in front of you, and then proceed with the upward mountain. In this pose, you will bring your palms above your head and allow them to touch each other. Breathe deeply throughout these poses. Keeping your hands like that, slowly bend sideways at your waist, first to the left and then to the right. Only bend far enough to feel a slight stretch. This is the crescent pose. After this, we will go into the goddess pose. Take a step so that your feet are shoulder-width apart and turned outwards. Squat down low so that your knees are right above your ankles, creating a rectangular shape. Extend your arms out away from your body and bring them to a prayer mudra, with your thumb touching your middle finger, and your hands facing upwards.

Next, you should do the star pose. For this pose, stand up

and open your legs slightly. Hold your arms out to the side, in line with your shoulders, so that you create a star shape with your body. From there, bend at the waist and reach down, touching your left arm to your left foot without bending your knees, creating the triangle pose. When your left arm is down, your right arm will remain extended upwards and vice versa. Then, bring the second arm down to also touch that foot, to create the pyramid pose. From that pose, you can then bend your right knee back to touch the ground, extending the leg slightly. Your right foot and knee should be touching the ground, while your left leg should be bent in front of you with the knee facing upwards. Your arms should be stretched above your head, as you look up at your hands.

Our next pose involves a wide legged squat over the left leg. From the position you are in, bring your arms from above your head and all the way down touching the floor. Extend your right leg outwards from the right side of your body with your toes pointing up. Your left leg should be crouched in front of you. Rotate your left leg to the left side. In the end, this pose should have your palms pressed to the floor, your right leg extended with your toes pointing up, and your left leg folded to the side underneath your body.

Then do the whole routine on your other side, this time with your right foot. As you can imagine, you will follow the exact same pattern of poses on the opposite side, but in reverse order! Begin with the pyramid pose, the triangle pose, and the star pose, then the goddess pose and the crescent pose, before completing the cycle with the mountain pose. Finally, bring both your palms facing each other to the height of your chest and give thanks to the Moon, by repeating, *Namaste*.

This is a magnificent way for you to relax and become fully aligned with the Moon. The best way to perform this sequence of yoga poses is, of course, during the full moon and the new moon, but you are free to do this on a daily basis, if you feel like there is some harmony missing. Whenever you wish to relax and let go of the tension, reevaluating your life and bringing balance, Moon salutations can help you a great deal. Perform them mindfully and be grateful to the Moon for enabling you to reach your goals and welcome your blessings.

After that, you can prepare yourself some herbal or chamomile tea, and sit comfortably at your spiritual altar. Avoid any blue light for at least an hour before bedtime, and instead focus on your personal growth. Visualize your intentions, write in your journal and track your mood. Find things in your day that have made you feel good about yourself and reflect on them! You should be proud of your accomplishments, exuding positivity and elevating your frequencies. If you spend those last moments of your day comparing yourself to others and feeling lacking, then this is what you are going to project to the world.

AFTERWORD

You have made it to the end of this book and this fills me with great joy and satisfaction! I am sure that you have learned a lot about the power of the Moon and its cherished energy, and have gained a new, more spiritual perspective on life! In this book, I have put all my love into creating something that speaks right to your heart and allows you to claim your birthright. You have been blessed as a human being with a wealth of things, if you only reach out and grab them. The Moon will be right there by your side, whether you can see it or not. It is supporting you, helping you reach your goals and enjoy life exactly how you deserve.

In the book, I have explained the different moon phases and the way each of them affects you in your life. As soon as you fully comprehend the way the Moon works in combination with the rest of the cosmos, you will be able to unfold those mystical secrets of the universe and use them to your advantage! I have talked about the zodiac signs and how your astrological birth chart can influence your life on so many levels, provided that you know where to look. Next, I have referred to the emblematic Law of Attraction that dictates your life and defines what you receive from the world around you.

It has been a wonderful adventure, laying out these guided meditations that you can practice throughout the different moon phases. Some of them should be performed during the new moon, while others are ideal for the full moon, or even all throughout the lunar cycle. Just make sure to immerse yourself in the meditation and give your heart and soul into setting realistic intentions, so that you can watch them grow and become your new reality. Welcome change into your life, and be open and receptive to those glorious blessings. Have faith in the process, because it is based on the eternal power of the Moon and its overwhelming energy!

Finally, I have included a morning ritual you can perform every day to enhance the effectiveness of the Moon energy in your life. A nighttime ritual is also available, in order to give thanks to the Moon and increase your mental clarity, while letting go of the tension and releasing all negativity before going to sleep. If you are consistent and dedicate time to performing these rituals, then you will welcome change and see your entire life transform, finally forming exactly the way you have been dreaming of. I am looking forward to communicating with you in my other books as well, filling the missing pieces of spirituality one by one.

By taking initiative and choosing this book, you have already completed the first and most important step towards improving your life! You had an amazing idea and you now have all the things you need, in order to make wonders happen. I am confident that you are going to achieve greatness sooner than you have ever anticipated. There are so many wonderful things waiting for you to open and receive in your life! You are ready, and it is time to welcome abundance, pure joy, and success supercharged by lunar energy. Aren't you excited about what comes next? Just reach out and claim what has been destined for you by the wise universe! I believe in you and you are entitled to all the blessings of the world. So go on, conquer them, and enjoy every moment of your life from now on... you deserve it!

REFERENCES

Ackerman, C. E. (2018, May 2). *Self-Fulfilling Prophecy in Psychology: 10 Examples and Definition (+PDF)*. PositivePsychology.com. https://positivepsychology.com/self-fulfilling-prophecy/

adege. (2018). *Lunar Eclipse Blood Moon Full* [Photograph]. Pixabay. https://pixabay.com/photos/lunar-eclipse-blood-moon-moon-3568801/

Bessi. (2015). *Tree Lake Stars* [Photograph]. Pixabay. https://pixabay.com/photos/tree-lake-stars-reflection-water-838667/

Candiix. (2018). *Moon Couple Blue* [Photograph]. Pixabay. https://pixabay.com/photos/moon-couple-blue-love-in-love-3059324/

Choi, C. Q. (2017, September 8). *Moon Facts: Fun Information About the Earth's Moon*. Space.com. https://www.space.com/55-earths-moon-formation-composition-and-orbit.html

Comfreak. (2016). *Earth Moon Space* [Photograph]. Pixabay. https://pixabay.com/illustrations/earth-moon-space-space-travel-1151659/

DanaTentis. (2017). *Woman Brunette Lying Down* [Photograph]. Pixabay. https://pixabay.com/photos/woman-brunette-lying-down-rest-2003647/

Dropic, A. (2018). *Science Nature Moon* [Photograph]. Pixabay. https://pixabay.com/photos/science-nature-moon-mountain-3191080/

enriquelopezgarre. (2020). *Landscape Cave Moon* [Photograph]. Pixabay. https://pixabay.com/photos/landscape-cave-moon-twilight-night-5563684/

enriquelopezgarre. (2020). *Landscape Night Star* [Photograph]. Pixabay. https://pixabay.com/photos/landscape-night-star-phases-5186058/

fietzfotos. (2020). *Moon Night Plastic* [Photograph]. Pixabay. https://pixabay.com/photos/moon-night-plastic-crescent-5224745/

Free-Photos. (2014). *Tea Cup Rest* [Photograph]. Pixabay. https://pixabay.com/photos/tea-cup-rest-calm-afternoon-381235/

Free-photos. (2015). *Milky Way Stars Man* [Photograph]. Pixabay. https://pixabay.com/photos/milky-way-stars-man-silhouette-1023340/

GabbyConde. (2020). *Crystals Selenite Stones* [Photograph]. Pixabay. https://pixabay.com/photos/crystals-selenite-stones-stone-4831221/

Grover, N. (2021, January 27). *Lunar cycle has distinct effect on sleep, study suggests*. The Guardian. https://www.theguardian.com/lifeandstyle/2021/jan/27/lunar-cycle-has-distinct-effect-on-sleep-study-suggests

Hickey, H. (2016, January 29). *Moon's tidal forces affect amount of rainfall on Earth*. UW News. https://www.washington.edu/news/2016/01/29/phases-of-the-moon-affect-amount-of-rainfall/

KELLEPICS. (2020). *Fantasy Moon Girl* [Photograph]. Pixabay. https://pixabay.com/illustrations/fantasy-moon-girl-night-bank-5316369/

Lopez Simpson, S. (2017, October 6). *9 Habits to Manifest Your Dreams Using the Law of Attraction*. Mindbodygreen. https://www.mindbodygreen.com/0-16150/9-habits-to-manifest-your-dreams-using-the-law-of-attraction.html

mcbeaner. (2017). *Aurora Moon Scotland* [Photograph]. Pixabay. https://pixabay.com/illustrations/aurora-moon-scotland-beach-2069242/

MiraCosic. (2015). *Astrology Divination Chart* [Photograph]. Pixabay. https://pixabay.com/photos/astrology-divination-chart-993127/

mistockshop. (2016). *Planner Journal Notebook* [Photograph]. Pixabay. https://pixabay.com/photos/planner-journal-notebook-organizer-1873485/

Sinnott, R. W. (2017, September 14). *Find the Phase of the Moon*. Sky & Telescope. https://skyandtelescope.org/observing/the-phase-of-the-moon/

spiritiiiii. (2017). *Moon Full Moonlight* [Photograph]. Pixabay. https://pixabay.com/photos/moon-full-moon-moonlight-super-moon-2285627/

terimakasiho. (2019). *Chest Treasure Pirate* [Photograph]. Pixabay. https://pixabay.com/photos/chest-treasure-pirate-money-box-4051166/

vitavalka. (2015). *Clock Historical Prague* [Photograph]. Pixabay. https://pixabay.com/photos/clock-historical-prague-city-signs-1096054/

Willgard. (2018). *Dreams Heaven Stairs Fantasy* [Photograph]. Pixabay. https://pixabay.com/photos/dreams-heaven-stairs-fantasy-woman-3745156/

World History Edu. (2021, May 4). *Khonsu: Ancient Egyptian God of the Moon and Time*. World History Edu. https://www.worldhistoryedu.com/khonsu-ancient-egyptian-god-of-the-moon-and-time/

PLEASE LEAVE A REVIEW ON AMAZON

From the bottom of my heart, thank you for reading my book. I truly hope that it helps you on your spiritual journey and to live a more empowered and happy life. Would you be kind enough to leave an honest review for this book on Amazon? I would be ecstatic to read your feedback and it could impact the lives of others across the globe, giving them hope and power. I read **every** review I receive and each one helps me become the best writer I can be.

Thank you and good luck,

Angela Grace

JOIN OUR COMMUNITY

Why not join our Facebook community and discuss your spiritual path with like-minded seekers?

We would love to hear from you!

Go here to join the Ascending Vibrations community: ***bit.ly/ascendingvibrations***

CLAIM YOUR FREE AUDIOBOOK

DOWNLOAD THE *'SPIRITUAL CLEANSING'* AUDIOBOOK INSTANTLY FOR FREE

If you love listening to audio books on-the-go, I have great news for you. You can download the audiobook version of *'Spiritual Cleansing'* for **FREE** just by signing up for a **FREE** 30-day audible trial! Turn the page for more details!

Audible trial benefits

As an audible customer, you'll receive the below benefits with you 30-day free trial:

• Free audible copy of this book

• After the trial, you will get 1 credit each month to use on any audiobook

• Your credits automatically roll over to the next month if you don't use them

• Choose from over 400,000 titles

• Listen anywhere with the audible app across multiple devices

• Make easy, no hassle exchanges of any audiobook you don't love

• Keep your audiobooks forever, even if you cancel your membership

• And much more

Click the links below to get started:

Go here for audible US:

bit.ly/spiritualcleansinglisten

Go here for audible UK:

bit.ly/spiritualcleansinglistenuk

Manufactured by Amazon.ca
Bolton, ON

21301810R00072